The World-Shattering Ministry of Jesus

Anne B. Crumpler
and John O. Gooch

ABINGDON PRESS
Nashville

THE WORLD-SHATTERING MINISTRY OF JESUS

by Anne B. Crumpler and John O. Gooch

This book is printed on recycled, acid-free paper.

ISBN 0-687-09072-5

ISBN 978-0-687-09072-3

07 08 09 10—10 9 8 7 6

MANUFACTURED IN THE UNITED STATES OF AMERICA

Contents

Meet the Writers

Anne B. Crumpler comes from a long line of preachers, teachers, and writers; she learned theology, Bible, and English grammar over the dinner table. She also has a Bachelor of Arts in Philosophy from Chatham College and a Master of Religious Education from St. Meinrad School of Theology. Anne is the writer of Chapters 2, 6, and 7.

Anne has been an assistant editor in the Department of Youth Publications, The United Methodist Publishing House, and is presently a freelance writer and editor. Anne is also a contract editor for *The Upper Room Daily Devotional Guide* and for *Devo-Zine.* She has written Bible lessons for *Mature Years*, articles for *Devo-Zine* and *Alive Now*, devotions for *The Upper Room Disciplines* and *365 Meditations for Families*, sermon helps for *What Difference Would It Make?* and study guides for Lent offered online by The Upper Room.

Anne lives in Nashville, Tennessee, with her husband, David. They have two spectacular children, Rachel and Benjamin.

John O. Gooch is a husband, father, brother, grandfather, uncle, and friend. His chief delight is in family (whom he has not left for the sake of Jesus). In addition, Dr. Gooch is a retired member of the Missouri East Annual Conference of The United Methodist Church, a church historian, Rotarian, and active writer and youth minister. From childhood, John has been fascinated by the Bible and the message it carries. Each year, he says, he learns something more about the Scriptures that excites him all over again. John is the writer of Chapters 1, 3, 4, and 5.

Dr. Gooch holds the Ph.D. in Historical Theology from St. Louis University, an M.Div. from Garrett-Evangelical Theological Seminary, and an A.B. from Central Methodist University. His most recent books are *Circuit Riders to Crusades: Essays in Missouri Methodist History* and *Claiming the Name: A Theological and Practical Overview of Confirmation* for Abingdon Press.

He and his wife, Beth, live in Liberty, Missouri, where they are active in the Liberty United Methodist Church.

A Word of Welcome

Welcome to THE WORLD-SHATTERING MINISTRY OF JESUS, a study of some of the teachings of Jesus that shook up his hearers and the status quo of his peers. There are two writers for this volume, and each has used his or her own voice in bringing to light the meaning and application of some of Jesus' most difficult pronouncements. In these chapters you will find

- a description of the world in which Jesus and his disciples conducted their ministry and how Jesus identified himself at the outset of that ministry;
- a commentary on the nature of sin and how Jesus came particularly to call to salvation those whom society labeled as sinners and outcasts;
- Jesus' "cleansing of the Temple" and the implications and consequences of that challenge to the authority of the religious leaders;
- the challenge Jesus posed to the interpretation of Scripture in his day and how that investment into a deeper meaning urged his hearers to a more faithful life;
- ways in which Jesus challenged and threatened the existing social order (or "system") by reaching out to persons who were considered unclean and welcoming them into the community and the Kingdom;
- a radical reinterpretation of the use and possession of wealth;
- Jesus' call to a life of discipleship and how relinquishment of cherished ways of life bring transformation and liberty.

We invite you to delve deeply into this study of Jesus' challenging teachings and pray that you will find a blessing in it.

How to Use This Resource

We hope you enjoy participating in this study, either on your own or with a group. We offer these hints and suggestions to make your study a success.

THE WORLD-SHATTERING MINISTRY OF JESUS is a self-contained study with all the teaching/learning suggestions conveniently located on or near the main text to which they refer. They are identified with the same heading (or a close abbreviation) as the heading in the main text. In addition to your Bible, all you need to have a successful group or individual study session is provided for you in this book.

Some special features are provided as well, such as the **Bible 301** activities in the teaching helps. We usually think of the "101" designation as the beginning level; these "301" designations prompt you to dig deeper. In these instances you will be invited to look up Scriptures, key words, or concepts in a Bible dictionary, commentary, or atlas. On occasion, an added book or resource is cited that may be obtained from your local library or perhaps from your pastor. Those resources are extras; your study will be enriched by these added sources of information, but it is not dependent on them.

This study is intentionally invitational. In the closing activity, you are invited to give prayerful consideration to the concepts and insights from the chapter and your experience in the class session and to offer your own spoken prayers with and for others. We trust you will participate in these activities as you feel comfortable and that you will use them as a challenge to grow more confident with prayer and with your covenant with Jesus Christ.

Session One

Galilee of the Gentiles

Session Focus

Jesus lived within several cultures and dealt with people from all parts of society.

Session Objective

To establish the historical and cultural setting in which Jesus lived and to see how that setting led him to cause trouble for the authorities of his day.

Session Preparation

Be aware of "I didn't know that" points throughout the text. Ask yourself if "troublemaker" is an image of Jesus with which you feel comfortable. Have on hand a Bible atlas and a Bible dictionary.

Choose from among these activities and discussion starters to plan your lesson.

Get Started

Think about the image of a "troublemaker." What does that mean? What elements of that definition apply to Jesus? Had you ever thought about Jesus as a troublemaker before?

Galilee of the Gentiles

What kinds of religious/social communities would welcome the image of Jesus as a troublemaker? Most of us probably prefer a Jesus who is gentle and comforting. But the Jesus of the Gospels was, in fact, a "troublemaker"; and the faith communities for whom the Gospels were written rather seemed to like that. Why? To help us answer that question, we will look first at the political, economic, and social world into which Jesus was born, and then look at Luke 1:46-53.

Galilean Culture and Economy

Jesus grew up in "Galilee of the Gentiles." There were four characteristics of Galilean society that are important for our study. First, there was a conflict between Hellenic and Hebrew customs and tradition. Greek (Hellenic) culture believed it represented the highest ideal of humanity and that one had to be a Hellenist if one were to be a complete human being. (Naturally, Jews believed the same thing about Jewish/Hebrew culture.) In Galilee, Greek was the language of business and political discourse. Jesus and the disciples probably knew at least basic Greek in order to function in the world. The cultural situation was very similar to what we experience in the United States at the beginning of the twenty-first century. The

Christian community experiences a cultural collision between "secular humanism" on the one extreme and strict fundamentalism on the other, with religious gradations and shadings in between. We discover as a religious community that it isn't easy to live in a clash of cultures (in which humanism and Christianity are but two approaches to life).

Second, economic life was easier in Galilee than elsewhere in Palestine. Galilee was, and is today, the breadbasket of Israel. The warm, rich volcanic soil makes for bountiful crops. Because the soil is so dark and absorbs so much heat from the sun, crops are earlier in Galilee than in Judea, even though it is farther north. Major trade routes ran through Galilee. The "Way of the Sea," the major highway between the empires of Mesopotamia and Egypt, for example, passed through Capernaum. This level of travel opened up economic opportunities for what we would call service industries. In addition, the fish taken from the Lake of Galilee were salted or dried and shipped widely across the Middle East.

In all this prosperity there was also a great deal of poverty and economic oppression. At least half of the income of a Galilean family went to taxes. Some of this went to the Temple, but the majority went to Rome. These taxes were deeply resented, and tax collectors, such as Matthew (Levi) and Zacchaeus, were hated by the population.

In his parables Jesus talked about the economic and social problems caused by absentee landlords (who cared not for the people, but for potential profits); small farmers; "hired men"; and day laborers with no steady employment. Absentee ownership was a major source of economic hardship for the Galilean peasantry, whose lives were always

Galilee ■

Think about what makes your own culture unique (language, values, relationships, society expectations and hierarchies, and so on). What cultural forces are brought to bear against persons, ideas, practices, or values that attempt to operate counter to the culture?

What power do language and economy carry in shaping values, expectations, and behaviors?

Consider the cultural and economic identity of Galilee. Review this section of the main text to be sure you have a working understanding of the time in which Jesus lived.

Bible 301 □

Using a Bible atlas or the maps in your study Bible, locate greater Palestine. If you have a relief map or other maps that indicate rainfall, for example, compare Galilee geographically with areas surrounding it. Locate a map with trade routes to understand the strategic location of Galilee.

In small groups, either adapt a parable or create a new one that Jesus might tell today using cultural images and metaphors that are familiar to you.

difficult. Often they saw what little they earned go to rents or were forced off the land completely. We wonder what kind of parables Jesus would tell today about issues such as the minimum wage, adequate health care for all persons, underemployment, "golden parachutes," and other economic phenomena.

Bible 301: Roman Oppression

In small groups, use a Bible dictionary to learn more about Judas Maccabeus, Herod the Great, Judas ben Hezekiah, Judas the Galilean, and the Zealots. Discuss how the history of these revolts, both successful and failed, might have colored the hopes and expectations concerning the Messiah.

Next, look up messiah. *How is the Messiah understood? What was the Messiah to do and be? Why would the Messiah be a threatening figure for the prevailing powers in Palestine?*

Roman Oppression

Third, the political situation was strongly anti-Roman, except among a few at the top of society. In the time of Jesus, the memory of a great war of independence fought against an oppressor who was actively pushing Hellenism was still fresh. The names of Judas Maccabeus and his brothers were ranked as great heroes, just as we would rank Washington, Jefferson, Franklin, and other leaders in our great revolutionary generation. The spirit of independence was still alive and expressed itself more than once in great revolts against Roman authority. When Herod the Great died (4 B.C.), there was a revolt in Galilee under the leadership of Judas ben Hezekiah. Some two thousand rebels were crucified after the revolt was put down. Ten years later, when Jesus was about fifteen, another revolt occurred under Judas the Galilean. After this revolt, the Romans lined the main highway through Galilee with crosses. Jesus would only have had to climb the hill behind Nazareth to see the terrible cost of revolt.

One of the "parties" in the Galilee of Jesus' day was the Zealots, and their extreme wing, the Sicarii. The Zealots were the revolutionary underground, those who were watching and waiting for the day when they could raise the standard of revolt and drive out the Romans. At least one of Jesus' disci-

What were the prevailing issues that created a longing for someone to "fix things"? List all of the factors that would have had to be addressed for Jesus to "fix things" as an integrated political, religious, and kingly figure. (Think about the entire infrastructure of the Roman and Jewish worlds—competing religious understandings; the gap in power and distribution of wealth; and so on.) What would have compelled persons to think that this relatively unknown Jesus was the one to provide relief from Rome or anything else?

ples was a Zealot (Simon); some scholars have argued that others were, as well.

Certainly, in Jesus' day, there was a deep longing for a messiah of David, one who would cleanse the land of Romans and Hellenists and reestablish the independence Israel had known under David and under Judas Maccabeus. Whenever the crowds hailed Jesus as "Son of David," they were expressing this kind of hope. The fact that Jesus allowed that kind of acclamation even to occur marked him (in the eyes of the authorities) as a dangerous man whom they needed to watch.

Read Matthew 5:21-48 with special attention toward verses 38-48. In pairs, small groups, or individually, find a way to illustrate or demonstrate the "before and after" teachings of Jesus. (Draw, debate, journal, act out, set in contemporary situations, and paraphrase.) Then examine how these reversals and new nuances of old teachings would have influenced Jesus' hearers. How do they influence you?

Galilee (along with Judea) was an occupied province. When Jesus said, "If a man forces you to go with him one mile, go with him two" (see Matthew 5:41), he was referring to the custom that allowed Roman soldiers to commandeer any native to carry his pack or other gear for a mile. This kind of exploitation was just one reason why Rome was thoroughly hated.

One of the ways in which Jesus was a revolutionary and a troublemaker was in his teaching about dealing with the Romans. Imagine, in a situation of foreign oppression and hatred, saying, "Love your enemies and pray for those who persecute you" (Matthew 5:43-46). Imagine, in a similar setting, saying that the kingdom of God is characterized by reconciliation and loving relationships.

Longing for a Messiah

In pairs, or in the privacy of a personal journal, describe what your greatest religious or spiritual longing is. How does your relationship with Jesus Christ fulfill that longing? If it doesn't, try to determine

Longing for a Messiah

Fourth, the longing for a messiah was also a religious hope. Messiah was God's chosen one, who would bring freedom to God's people. The hope of a messiah was a mixture of religion and politics. Some longed for a strictly political messiah, who would establish an earthly kingdom. Some longed for a

why. (This is not an occasion to berate yourself for being somehow insufficient or "not faithful enough.")

Think about the ways you sense God's presence or find yourself drawn to the divine (through music, poetry, service to others, work that facilitates justice or meets human need, for example). How do you see God leading or "wooing" you?

Read Luke 1:26-38. What picture of Mary emerges? Then read Luke 1:46-55, the Magnificat or "Song of Mary," and talk about the attributes of the *anawim*. How would Mary's song be a word of encouragement to them? to the *anawim* of today?

priestly messiah, who would reestablish right worship. Some longed for a new prophet like Moses, and some longed for a combination of two or more of the above.

Messianism was in the air, and the threat of death was not a deterrent to still another potential messiah raising the standard of revolt. Rome was uncomfortable with messiahs, so Jesus was clearly in danger when his followers began to acclaim him as the Messiah.

Against the political and social background of the first century, we can now look at the "Song of Mary," Luke 1:46-55. Scholars identify this as a hymn on the *anawim*, the poor ones who were the core of the Jewish-Christian church. *Anawin* were not only the economically poor. They were the "afflicted" and "bowed down," those who were oppressed by the rich. In sum, the term refers to all those who were unfortunate, lowly, sick, or downtrodden in contrast to the rich, the arrogant, the ones who felt they did not need God. Luke put this song in Mary's mouth because she was one of the *anawim* and because his church considered Mary to be the ideal disciple, the one who spoke their own hopes and longings.

Luke 1:46-50 praises God for divine favor to Mary (and by extension to the poor). God is the "Mighty One," whose name is holy. God is a God of mercy. These were the attributes most valued by the *anawim*, who were dependent on God for everything. The "promise he made to our ancestors" (1:55) is a reminder of the covenant relationship between God and Israel, begun with Abraham and continued through Abraham's descendants. At the heart of the covenant is a relationship of love between God and the people that allows God to be active on their behalf.

Bible 301 ☐

Find in your music and worship resources hymns or other liturgy based on Luke 1:46-55, such as "The First One Ever," "My Soul Gives Glory to My God," or "Tell Out, My Soul." Sing or read one or more of these together. How does this worshipful presentation help you receive the blessing of the Magnificat?

Covenant Concern for the Poor

The Hebrew concept of covenant also included a strong sense of justice—caring for the poor, the oppressed, all those who could not care for themselves. This was more than just works of mercy for the poor. Justice implied that the king would personally intervene (as God's representative) and change the system so the poor would have the opportunity to provide the basic necessities of life for their families. The king would stand by the side of the oppressed and persons on the margins of society, ensuring they became a part of the mainstream of life and culture.

Justice for the poor was essential to God's people, even if that meant the rich and powerful lost some of their wealth and power. The *anawim* knew that the Messiah would "turn the world upside down" to bring that kind of justice for the poor. They saw the coming of the Messiah in Jesus, and their hopes are reflected in Mary's song of praise.

The acts for which Mary praises God are those that "turn the world upside down." God scatters the proud, brings down the powerful, lifts up the lowly, fills the hungry with good things, and sends the rich away empty (see Luke 1:51-53). Luke, looking back from the Resurrection, put on Mary's lips the hopes of the community that longed for God's justice in the world. Luke says clearly that the power of God was involved in the conception of Jesus to bring about the change for which the poor ones hoped.

Covenant Concern

Review the text on justice and on the king's responsibility for the poor. How would you describe a just society for the people of Jesus' day? Imagine yourself as part of that society with a rough approximation of how your work would translate into that society (this will require imagination!). Into what part of the social stratum do you fit? What would have to change, if anything, for you to be "part of the mainstream of life and culture"?

If your position and occupation (businessperson, teacher, or other professional) placed you among the upper classes, how, for that day, would a loss of your own wealth or even sharing of your resources with others influence your life? If you were among those with no land, what would it mean for you to receive justice?

Consider your present place in society. Are you a "have" or a "have not"? What would your worldview be if Jesus "turned your world upside down"? Would this be a hopeful or a discouraging change? Why?

Hope for Those of "Low Degree"

Today, the church in the United States is often a church of the affluent and comfortable, not of the poor. If we are among the well off, would we want to praise God for

Hope for the Lowly

Does God have, as some have suggested, a "preferential option for the poor"? Review Luke 1:46-55. What does Mary's song say about God? about government? If justice is an important element of the covenant, are there parallel implications for our political and economic systems today? Is the kind of justice we find in Mary's song an important part of grace?

turning our economic and social world upside down? What does our answer to that question suggest about the way we see God working? about the kinds of people for whom we see God having a special concern? Is it "me and my wife, my son John and his wife, us four and no more"? Or is God's concern primarily for those who have not? How we answer that question will help determine just how much of a "troublemaker" Jesus is for us.

Mary's song is about the hopes of the poor. For what do the poor in your community hope? How could you find out? If the song is correct about who God is and what God wants, then what do we need to do about it?

The parallels we find in Luke 1:51-53 are also expressions of the hopes of the *anawim*. There we find the mighty over against those of "low degree"; the hungry over against the rich; and those who fear God (1:50) over against the proud and arrogant. These are the opposites that God will change in the new world of the Messiah.

This hope is expressed in the language structure Luke used in this passage. The Greek verbs refer to a definite action in the past; that is, the salvation that was brought about through the death and resurrection of Jesus. The Passion event was the supreme sign of God's power and the strength of God's arm when sin, death, and the devil were overthrown and the power they had over humanity was destroyed.

Look at the contrast between the Crucifixion as it would probably have been experienced at the time and how it was understood a generation later when Luke wrote his Gospel. Read Deuteronomy 21:22-23. The community of faith would have seen Jesus' crucifixion as a curse, something defiling. Try to imagine a current situation that would engender a similar kind of despair or hopelessness.

The contrast in Luke's retrospective writing with the way the event was experienced at the time could not have been greater. Then it seemed only that Jesus was dead, along with the hopes of his followers. Worse than that, Jesus had been crucified. Hebrew law clearly said that anyone "hanged on a tree" was cursed by God (Deuteronomy 21:22-23). In that moment, death was triumphant, sin reigned, and the followers of Jesus were in despair. But, on the third day, God raised Jesus from the dead. Death was trampled underfoot, and sin lost its power.

Luke looked back through this supreme example of scattering the proud and mighty and interpreted the conception of Jesus in its light.

So, Luke put these words in Mary's mouth not only to make a christological statement (who is Jesus, the Christ?); he also placed them on the lips of Mary, a part of the *anawim*. The words were an accurate reflection of her own beliefs and commitments as well as a song of praise for the mighty acts of God on behalf of the poor.

Indeed, looking at Mary's song through the eyes of the *anawim*, the "poor ones" of the early Jerusalem church, helps us better understand the song. For we, too, look back at Mary's pregnancy and the feelings she had about it, through the eyes of Jesus' life and ministry, death and resurrection. That is the only way we can see it. It was, in fact, the only way the early church could see it. The challenge for us in reading the text is whether we can overcome our own wealth and power enough to enter into the experience and insight of the early church.

Then look at that situation through the lens of the Resurrection. How is it different? How would Mary's song, anticipating great things of God, change your perspective?

Then look the situation as if you had been a crucifier. What would you be thinking and feeling about Mary's song?

The Anointed Servant

Luke 4:16-21 gives us insight into the economic, social, and religious world of the early church and of Jesus himself. This is the record of Jesus' only sermon at Nazareth. He read from Isaiah 61:1-2a, a song first sung in the days after the Exile in Babylon when God's people were struggling to discover their mission and purpose. What did it mean to be the people of God? By Jesus' day, this song had (by at least part of the people) been identified with the promised Messiah. Look at what it says about the mission of God's people, whether understood collectively or individually. They are filled with the Spirit of

The Anointed Servant

Read Isaiah 61, a passage that describes the "year of the Lord's favor." This passage presented to the exiled Hebrews a glorious portrait of better days in a restored Zion (Jerusalem). At the heart of this restoration was the redemption of a repentant nation, chastened and forgiven.

Imagine one situation of "exile" that was a consequence of your own poor choices and for which you have repented. Write your own song of celebration for God's grace and restoration. Use the tune to a favorite hymn or song and add your own lyrics or simply create your own poem or litany.

Bible 301 ☐

Look up anointed one *in a Bible dictionary and read at least a few of the Scriptures to which the dictionary refers. What is the role of the anointed one as God's agent?*

Read Luke 4:16-21. Who is "me" in this passage? Why does God's spirit "anoint" people? What was the specific mission of the anointed one? Is that mission still relevant for the church today? If it is, what do we need to do about it?

Bible 301: Proclaiming Jubilee ☐

Look up Jubilee *in a Bible dictionary and the Scriptures to which the definition refers. How would you describe the Jubilee in your own words?*

What would happen to our social and economic system

God. They are anointed, that is, consecrated for a special purpose. The great danger for the church is always that we will think being anointed means we're important and God really likes us. All we have to do is sit back and enjoy God's favor. But that is not what Luke—or Jesus—had in mind.

The anointing here is a sign that the servant to whom Isaiah referred (either an individual or the people as a whole) had been chosen to live out the spirit of prophecy, to proclaim good news. Anointing is for service, not comfort: God's people are sent. They bear a commission, first, to preach good news to the poor. There are many persons who are sure of their own power and position, even of their own righteousness, and do not think they need the saving power of God. The servant did not come for those people. He came for the poor.

The servant is to proclaim liberty to the captives. The "captives" are not necessarily prisoners in the local jail or prisoners of war or even exiles. In Hebrew "liberty to the captives" could mean the freeing of slaves (see Jeremiah 34:8-9; Isaiah 42:22; 45:13). It could also mean the liberation of the year of Jubilee (Leviticus 25:8-55). This highly honored, but seldom practiced law was intended as a built-in restoration of justice and equality in the economic world.

Proclaiming Jubilee

The Jubilee came every fiftieth year. In it, no one planted or harvested, but ate only what fields and vineyards produced naturally. More important, all sales and other exchanges of property were pro-rated from the Jubilee year, for when "the year of Jubilee is come," all property was to be returned to whoever owned it at the begin-

if we took seriously the year of Jubilee? What would change in your own economic and social situation? What would happen to your relationship with God?

How would you respond to the questions in the second paragraph of the main text?

Review the audience of Jesus' message in Luke 4; what Mary represented to Luke's audience; the disparity between Rome and Jewish Palestine and between the few members of the privileged classes and majority in the peasant class. How would Jesus be seen as a radical or a troublemaker and as a messiah?

Jesus strongly challenged the status quo, not to ravage with guilt, but to inspire a change of heart. What new things has Jesus' message in this lesson laid on your heart? How might you hear God calling you to repent and be renewed or restored?

ning of the fifty-year period. No one knows if this law was ever actually practiced, but the intent was clear. None of God's people was ever to be forced into permanent economic dependence or servitude. None of God's people was ever to be deprived of his family property permanently. The text that Jesus read was more than just a nice statement of ideals. It was a call to long-term, systemic, economic and social justice.

One suspects that, by the time Jesus reached this point in his reading, some of his listeners were already uncomfortable thinking about just what was being read—just as we get uncomfortable reading about it. What would happen to the economic system if lending agencies couldn't foreclose on property? Does this business about "liberty" mean that people on welfare, or the working poor who hang on to the edges of the economic miracle by their fingernails, could and should be set free from that misery, made full economic partners in American society? Who else in our society needs to be liberated? These are the kind of people for whom Jesus came—the very ones to whom the good news was proclaimed.

There is more. Isaiah reads "release to the prisoners," which is the Hebrew reading (Isaiah 61:1b). The Greek translation, which Luke was using, reads "recovery of sight to the blind" (see Luke 4:21). Since the Hebrew can also mean "opening of the eyes," either translation is possible. In either case, it is closely related to the idea of release to the captives and has deep roots in the idea of systemic social and economic justice.

Luke closes the quotation with the words, "to proclaim the year of the Lord's favor" (4:19). This refers to the idea of Jubilee, to the "Day of the Lord" as proclaimed by

Amos and the other eighth-century prophets, and to the coming of the Messiah.

This Has Been Fulfilled

As a result of your reflection, what is God calling you to do or to be? To what might you be called to commit your time, energy, passion, and soul?

Consider entering a covenant with your study group to support one another in living out your commitments.

This Has Been Fulfilled

After he finished the reading, Jesus sat down. This was the proper posture for a teacher. Unlike our educational system, where the professor stands in front of the classroom and lectures, Jewish rabbis sat down and the pupils stood. Then he said, "Today this scripture has been fulfilled in your hearing" (4:21). We understand that to mean that Jesus was claiming the Scripture was fulfilled in him. The statement itself, however, is ambiguous and could simply mean that God was doing something in their midst. But think about the implications!

Imagine, for a minute, that everything you've just read about economic and social justice is true and is a part of God's will for the world. Now imagine that the Son of God is standing in the pulpit of your church on Sunday morning, explaining this text to your congregation. Then he says, "In me, all that God wills for economic and social justice is coming true." This is a clear call for repentance to all who support an oppressive system. In him, Jesus claimed, anyone can turn away from exploitation, greed, power, and work toward righteousness and justice. In this new life, everyone—including the poor, all those on the margins of society, the homeless, the hungry, the sick—has a place at the table. To those entrenched in having and maintaining power this was, and is, a troubling vision. Jesus challenged the powerful and encouraged the *anawim*; just the thing to turn the world of his hearers upside down.

Close With Devotions

Together, pray that you will be open to what God wants you to learn and do as a result of this study. Ask for God's help in understanding, in making commitments, and in living out those commitments in the world.

Sing one of the hymns based on Luke 1:46-55 or use a prayer that you worked on earlier (see "The Anointed Servant").

Session Two

Jesus Saves Sinners

Session Focus

Jesus troubles us. By associating with "tax collectors and sinners," he challenges not only our understanding of social propriety but also our faith.

Session Objective

To experience the radical nature of Jesus' claim, "I have come to call not the righteous but sinners."

Session Preparation

Read through the chapter. Be aware of the ways Jesus challenges your faith and life. Have on hand a Bible dictionary and a copy of *Rembrant: Life of Christ* (Nashville: Thomas Nelson Publishers, 1995).

Choose from among these activities and discussion starters to plan your lesson.

Me? I'm a Good Person

Rate yourself on a scale from 1 to 10. Ten is basically a good person. One is a first-class sinner.

Look at the "profile" of how we may identify ourselves and our sins. Does

Me? I'm a Good Person

We sing hymns proclaiming God's grace and our sinfulness. Like reformed slave trader John Newton, we confess

> Amazing grace how sweet the sound
> that saved a wretch like me.

In hymns and prayers, we confess our sins. It's easy: "I am a sinner." If we're honest, we admit to confessing our sins with tongue in cheek. We're ordinary people; our needs are modest; our sins innocuous. We confess to a kind of general sinfulness; but we're short on particulars. We may ask forgiveness for temper, greed, doubt, but nothing really bad (which overlooks how insidious a sin our temper or greed can commit). Basically we're good people. We're sinners, yes; but we're not the worst sinners.

All of us "have sinned and fall short of the glory of God" (Romans 3:23), but some of us have obviously fallen farther than others. We wouldn't keep company with men who spend their days in cubicles feeding quarters into triple-X rated peep shows or women who murder their children. Our sins don't compare with the sins of gang-bangers or drug dealers or the slick purveyors of Internet porn. Some people are simply more sinful than others.

We make distinctions. There are sinners in general and then there are "real sinners."

this describe you? How would you describe a "real" sinner?

Jesus got in trouble because he associated with real sinners. Not only that, but he saved them. Read Matthew 9:9-13. Jesus ate and drank with "tax collectors and sinners." Not only did Jesus associate with sinners, he kept company with others who were on the margins of society.

What Is Sin? ■

Review the meaning of sin. Form teams and divide the chapters in Leviticus 17–26 among them. Each team should skim through the chapters to understand what the ancient Hebrews identified as manifestations of sin.

Read Exodus 19:1-20. The Ten Commandments were the core of all the rest of the related laws on sin and leading a life of holiness.

Bible 301 □

Use a Bible dictionary to research the meaning and purpose of holiness. *Keep in mind that one dimension of holiness is separation; a concept that would have been in the front of the Pharisees' minds.*

What Is Sin?

Sinners referred to people who did not conform to the requirements of the law. The most frequent Hebrew word designating "sin" conveyed the sense of "revolt" or "transgression," a deliberate rebellion against or defiance of God. Ultimately, all sin is considered an act of idolatry because the sinner places something—usually his or her own sense of importance or superiority—before God.

Humankind shows evidence of sin in many ways. Jesus' hearers would have understood the manifestations of sin to show themselves in falling short of the purity codes (see Leviticus 17–20, for example); in social transgressions, such as cheating or lying (as in Exodus 20:12-17); and in spiritual lapses (such as hating or envying one's neighbor).

In Jesus' day, as now, there were consequences for sin. Though we think differently now, the biblical peoples believed that illness was the result of sin, as demonstrated when Jesus' disciples asked whose sin was responsible for a man's congenital blindness (see John 9:1-3).

Though "sin" was narrowly defined as an idolatrous defiance of God's sovereignty, it was widely attributed to many who missed the mark socially, spiritually, legally, and physically. These sinners and outcasts found themselves on the margins of their society.

Biblical Sinners and Outcasts

Gentiles were considered sinners; they were the "un-chosen" and "un-holy." Samaritans, for example, were the descendants of the conquered Hebrews of the kingdom of Israel who intermarried with persons of other conquered nations whom the Assyrians transplanted to that region. Some commentaries suggest that *sinners* refers to "people of the land," secular people who loosely interpreted and halfway followed the laws of God. Sinners were disobedient or at best apathetic.

Persons who failed to maintain the holiness codes fell out of favor. Beyond the Ten Commandments, the Hebrew tradition included the Holiness Code (Leviticus 11–22), a collection of interpretations and specific applications of the law intended to keep the religious community pure and its members holy. This Code legislated a broad range of behavior, including diet, sexual relationships, etiquette, and worship.

Those who disobeyed the laws were outcasts, excluded from the religious community. They had committed incest or adultery. They were homosexual. They ate food that was unclean. They were sick or bleeding. They did not observe the sabbath. They practiced witchcraft. They were thieves. They were dishonest businessmen and farmers who did not leave food for the poor.

As previously mentioned, these sinners might also be sick in some way. We know that Jesus spent time with people who were hoping for a miracle. They were blind, deaf, lame, sick, dying. They were paralyzed and carried by friends. They were "leprous," marked by the lesions of skin disease, feared as contagious and shamed through social condemnation. They were mentally or emo-

Biblical Sinners

Return to Leviticus 17–26. On a big piece of poster paper, do a word web on holiness. Write "Holiness" in the center of the page; from there, draw out lines citing various areas in which the Hebrews were called to be holy based on the regulations in Leviticus. Draw out lines from the added areas to indicate specific regulations applied to that area of holiness (for example: holiness→diet→no pork).

Discuss what this concept of holiness means to the church and to you today.

Consider the role of sin in illness. Sinful choices and bad judgment can contribute to poor health. Christian Science practitioners, for example, regard disease as contrary to God's will for us and rely on holy behavior to combat illness. Does this in some way make sick people sinful? Discuss reasons for your response.

tionally ill; often misunderstood as "possessed" and, therefore, religiously terrifying. Jesus spent time with people who were outcasts because they were sick in body or spirit. They were desperate people hoping for a cure for their ailment and restoration to their community.

Read Matthew 9:9-13. Begin a list of sinners and outcasts. With whom was Jesus spending his time?

Tax collectors were both social and religious outcasts. Because they worked for the Roman Empire, tax collectors were living reminders that the Jews were oppressed people. Regional taxes were collected by contracting services within a particular region, usually to wealthy foreigners, who then hired local publicans. The local publicans were free to collect what they could, including exorbitant profits. We might not assume that every tax collector was a crook and a thief, but as a group, they were despised and distrusted.

Bible 301 ☐

Look up tax collector *or* publican *in a Bible dictionary. What more complete portrait emerges as to the kind of person Matthew might have been?*

You can perhaps imagine a modern-day Matthew scrabbling through the streets with a briefcase overflowing with money, knocking at the doors of old women in rags, who have nothing left. Tax collectors were hated by almost everyone. Yet Jesus called Matthew, a tax collector, and made him a disciple. Jesus spent time with outcasts.

Outcasts Today ■

Add to your list. Today, who are outcasts of society? Who are the people excluded from religious communities? Who are immoral? Who do we consider "less than Christian"?

We may indiscriminately lump together felons, addicts, mentally ill persons, and awkward teens as persons who are outcast

Outcasts Today

Who would Jesus associate with today? Who are the outcasts of society? We may judge indiscriminately, lumping together any and all who don't conform to a preset notion of acceptability or ability. The outcasts are street people, ragged and stinking of whiskey and sweat. They are heroin addicts, scrawny, with glazed eyes and fried brains. They are kids who are too fat or too smart or too pimply or too insecure to fit in. They are schoolyard bullies and kids who kill. They are per-

or marginalized; but what is the effect of this generalization? What is the effect if we simply call all of them sinners?

Consider the ministry of your Christian fellowship groups and church. Is everyone welcome as they are? Are they welcome if they change to conform to some set of measures? If so, what are the measures? What does that say about the identity and faithfulness of the group?

Recall the Holiness Code of Leviticus. Think about the (probably) unspoken holiness code of your church or other Christian fellowship groups. Write out what the code is and why it was established that way. What purpose does it serve? Does it serve to exclude or place barriers? Does it work? Would it please God? Explain.

sons shut out or marginalized because of handicapping conditions, mental illness, emotional turmoil. The outcasts are pimps and drug dealers. They are sleazy businessmen and con artists and dirty old men.

Who are people the church excludes or expels from the religious community? Of course, we say that everyone is welcome; but truth be told, too often people who are not "just like us" either fall or are shoved "through the cracks." How does a black/a native American/a Hispanic person feel walking into an all-white church? How do children, teenagers, and elderly adults feel when the church treats them as "pre- or post-people"? Is the weekday lunch program something we offer to "clients" who are never invited to or welcome in our community of faith?

Though we may phrase it differently, we often have our own "holiness code." We want to keep our churches pure and our church members holy. Holiness is commanded by God; it is a worthy goal. All who sin are liable to God's judgment. But judging who is holy (or who falls short) is God's work, not our own.

We may think of ourselves as resident aliens, communities of faith in a secular world. We pull out a Levitical law to judge persons or acts we consider repugnant, as in the case of homosexuality (Leviticus 18:22); but conveniently ignore other biblical injunctions that are themselves repugnant, such as the requirement of a man to marry and never divorce a virgin whom he has raped (Deuteronomy 22:28-29). Some of us condemn New Age, astrology, secular humanism, people of other faiths, and even other brands of Christianity. Many churches exclude people whose political views are too conservative or too liberal. Jesus not only came to save the "tax collectors and sinners"; he came to challenge us, when we think too highly of ourselves, to repent of our arrogance and to open our hearts to all. Just because we think of "them" as outcasts does not mean that we are righteous.

What's the Trouble?

Think again about Jesus' call of Matthew (9:9-13). Picture Jesus sitting with friends at a local restaurant, ordering a burger and fries, being a little rowdy, laughing, telling stories, joining in as one of the crowd.

The Pharisees were clearly upset. "Why does your teacher eat with tax collectors and sinners?" The Pharisees were learned and practiced in the law and were strict observers of ritual purity, sabbath observance, and food laws. They typically did not associate with people outside the law lest they be tempted. To be identified with sinners, with "the unclean," would make them unclean. So the Pharisees' question, "Why does Jesus eat with sinners?" was an accusation. Jesus, by associating with sinners, was defiling himself.

We are also concerned about associations. Consider: Parents ask questions about their children's friends. Are they good kids? Will they be a good influence? Christian families sometimes insist that their children only spend time with other Christians. They don't want their children getting in with a bad crowd.

The fact is that all of us are concerned about the people with whom we spend time. We consider how friends will affect us. Other people's thoughts, ideas, decisions, feelings, and behavior rub off on us. If we're with people who are prejudiced, we're apt to become more prejudiced. If we demonstrate bias, we may lead others into bias.

What's the Trouble?

Consider one of the dimensions of holiness as being separate. Since this is one of the hallmarks of the kind of life to which God called the Hebrews, why is it a surprise or disappointment that the Pharisees were upset with Jesus for his association with persons regarded as impure? Would we think it improper or cause for judgment for a devout Christian or Jew to insist on honoring the sabbath, for example, or to uphold their religious convictions concerning their behavior or dealings with other people? What is the issue with these Pharisees, then?

Bible 301

Look at Rembrandt's etching of Jesus' healing the sick (in Rembrandt: Life of Christ*; Nashville, Thomas Nelson Publishers, 1995; page 70).*

Consider: What is Jesus doing in the picture? How is he standing? How do you know he's Jesus? Is Rembrandt's picture like your picture of Jesus? Why? Why not? Does

Rembrandt capture the sense of the Scripture in Matthew 9:9-13? Why? Why not?

We worry about what other people will think of us. "I'll be nice to him, but I can't be his friend. What would people say?" The group we hang out with says a lot about who we are. We make assumptions about others based on the company they keep, and we are liable to the same kinds of assumptions.

So what about Jesus? If Jesus ate and drank with "tax collectors and sinners," what do we know about him? Was he an outcast? Were his friends a bad influence on him?

Discuss: How do you choose your friends? With whom would you choose not to associate? Why? How would you feel if members of your family spent their time with "tax collectors and sinners"?

Jesus also associated with Pharisees, Sadducees, and scribes. Even as a boy, he sat with the elders in the Temple, learning at their feet. The Pharisees are reported by Matthew's Gospel as being appalled by Jesus' choice of friends. Are we like these Pharisees who don't much like *our* Jesus hanging out with the wrong crowd?

Salvation for Them ■

Does Jesus save everyone; or does Jesus pick and choose, saving only the worst sinners? How does Matthew 9:13-16 influence an "us versus them" attitude?

One synonym (though incomplete) for *righteous* is *good person*. How do you feel when you hear Jesus say, "I have come to call not the righteous but sinners"? Who are the righteous?

Salvation for Them

Jesus was curt: "I have come to call not the righteous but sinners" (Matthew 9:13). If we take this to mean that Jesus saves only sinners and not the righteous, Jesus' words are a slap in the face. They are also ridiculous. Who are the righteous, but those who have already come to God, repentant and devoting their lives to God's will and service? Jesus came to save the sinner—to a life right with God.

When we create false distinctions or place faulty labels on ourselves and others and think that Jesus concurs, we run into trouble. If all this time we thought that Jesus came only for us (as if we are not sinners), that Jesus saves us from our "little" sins and calls us to be disciples, but not those we label as "real" sinners, we are sadly mistaken. Perhaps we pictured ourselves walking hand in hand with Jesus, sitting at his table, listening, soaking up his wisdom. So far, so good. But that pretty picture must also include those whom we would exclude—whoever we label as "tax collectors and sinners."

Jesus' response to the criticism of these Pharisees is that "those who are well have no need of a physician, but those who are sick" (9:12). We like to identify ourselves with the "well," when in reality, most of us are at least a little bit "sick." To continue the analogy, the radical urgency of physician Jesus' "emergency care" was to those in the most critical condition. We know that if Jesus came again to our towns, he'd spend more time in smoky bars and sleazy storefronts than in Christian homes and Sunday school classrooms.

Who are the "sick"? Do you identify yourself with the sick or the well? Why? What does it mean that Jesus came to the sick but not to the well? What does it mean to be well in this context?

The Gospel of Luke (6:20-26) spells it out:

"Blessed are you who are poor. . . .

"Blessed are you who weep now. . . .

"Blessed are you when people hate you, and when they exclude you, revile you, and defame you on account of the Son of Man. . . .

"But woe to you who are rich . . . full . . . laughing. . . .

"Woe to you when all speak well of you."

Bible 301 ☐

Read or sing together "There Is a Balm in Gilead" or other song about healing and wholeness. Or, turn to a favorite hymn on repentance and regeneration. How do the words and music convey a sense of God's presence and care for you and for others?

New Meanings of Salvation

The fact that Jesus ate and drank with tax collectors and sinners challenges our understandings of salvation.

New Meanings of Salvation ■

What does *salvation* mean to you? Salvation is an intensely personal event, but can we do it justice by thinking of it only as personal? How do you understand salvation beyond your personal relationship to God?

First, we tend to think of salvation as personal. Jesus saves individuals. We imagine walking alone in the garden with Jesus; we think of our souls flying away from this world to be one with the Lord. To save us, Jesus takes us out of down-to-earth communities and walks with us in quiet solitude.

The Scripture creates a different image of salvation. Jesus saw Matthew sitting in his tax booth. Jesus called him; Matthew followed. Jesus took him to a party where "many tax collectors and sinners came and were sitting with him and his disciples" (Matthew 9:10).

Think about this scene of Matthew sitting in the tax booth and modernize it. From whom do we avert our eyes and wish not to enter the Kingdom? Why?

We might also imagine this scene: Matthew was a tax collector, sitting alone on the outskirts of the city. Because of the assumptions about his occupation, he was despised, an outcast of society. People walked past his booth, pretending not to see him, avoiding his eyes. The religious thought he was not only outside the law, but outside the scope of God's love. No one wanted anything to do with a tax collector.

Bible 301 □

Consider the idea of salvation as a party. Look up other passages that have to do with the kingdom of God being likened to a great banquet, such as Luke 14:7-14. What does this tell us about our "place" at God's table and how to regard other "guests"?

But Jesus saw him and took him to dinner with friends. Salvation for Matthew was not only being with Jesus; it was also being brought into a community. The gospel is clear: Salvation is not a walk in a garden alone with the Lord. Salvation is a community event. Jesus saves us with other people. Once we were alone; saved, we are together with one another and with Jesus. One image of salvation is a party, with good food and drink and laughter—sheer joy.

Salvation by Grace

Salvation by Grace ■

Discuss the popular notion of "If you're good, you'll go to heaven; if you're bad, you'll go to hell." What do *goodness* and *badness* have to do with salvation? How would you describe *good* and *bad*?

Matthew the tax collector may have been viewed as "too bad" to be worthy of Jesus' attention, though

Second, we believe that God will save us if we're good. Granted the creeds of the church say otherwise: We are saved by God's grace. But despite official statements of doctrine, many Christians accept the popular notion, "If you're good, you'll go to heaven; if you're bad, you'll go to hell."

Because Matthew was a tax collector, we assume that he was not a good person. But we also believe that Jesus saw the good in people. On the surface, they may have been

clearly he wasn't. Can anyone be too good to need or too bad to be worthy to claim God's attention? Why?

outcasts of society; but somewhere in their hearts Jesus found the good. If Matthew were the stereotypical tax collector, it would be assumed that he had no integrity; that he had sold his soul for a profit; that he was dishonest, greedy. As such he would have been a businessman with no compassion who stole from the poor and kissed up to the powerful. In his society, Matthew was cast out of society as having no redeeming social value. On the divine scales of reward and punishment, Matthew was going straight to hell.

Explore Jesus' comment that he "desires mercy and not sacrifice." What does *sacrifice* mean in this context? How is mercy tied to salvation and what does that tell us about our responsibility to show mercy? We may think ourselves righteous, but we still receive God's mercy. In what ways do you see that demonstrated in your own life?

In what ways does the Scripture challenge your beliefs about salvation?

But Jesus saw him—regardless of his evil character (whether real or imagined)—and called him. Jesus took him to dinner with friends. Jesus saved him.

Jesus challenges our understanding of salvation: "Go and learn what this means, 'I desire mercy, not sacrifice' " (Matthew 9:13). When the Pharisees condemned the tax collectors and sinners, Jesus reminded them of God's mercy—God's amazing grace. God's mercy, says Jesus, is not based on the good we do. It is not meted out according to the law or according to community standards of piety or morality. God's love is undeserved, freely given even to all the Matthews of the world.

Salvation as Transformation

Read 2 Corinthians 5:16-19 and 1 Corinthians 15:42-44. What does it mean to be a new creation—not just to act differently or to feel new or to change to fresh attitudes—but to be a *new* creation? How is this possible?

Salvation as Transformation

Third, we understand salvation as transformation. Each of us becomes a new creation, designed along the lines of Jesus himself. Our sins are forgiven; in Jesus Christ, we become new people.

Certainly the Scripture supports our understanding. The apostle Paul says that we are "a new creation" (2 Corinthians 5:16-19), that in Christ, the perishable has become imperishable, dishonor is raised to glory,

Think about repentance as a turning from sin and toward God and as a determined effort to break down the self-erected barriers that stand between yourself and God. Then in two small groups read John 3:1-3 and Luke 18:18-23. What were the barriers? What are your barriers? With these two stories as examples, talk with a partner or write privately in what ways you might need to repent and what you can do to remove barriers between yourself and a life right with God.

Read Luke 19:1-10. What were the barriers that stood in Zacchaeus's way to a righteous life? We know that the tax collector Matthew left his office and became one of Jesus' inner circle, but we don't know what Zacchaeus did. Imagine a story about his new life. In turns add briefly to the Scripture story to describe Zacchaeus as a new creation. Keep going until everyone has had at least one opportunity to add something to the story. How might Zacchaeus's new story be your story?

weakness is changed to power (1 Corinthians 15:42-44). Being saved means being changed.

Some people think that repentance is a prerequisite to salvation. Repentance means being sorry for what we've done and changing. Other people say that change follows salvation. Because we are saved, we change.

In fact, Jesus calls people to repent. He told Nicodemus that he must be born again (John 3:1-3). He told the rich man to sell what he had and to give to the poor (Luke 18:18-23). Mark 1:15 says that Jesus came preaching, "Repent, and believe in the good news." Repentance means turning to God and removing the barriers that stand between us and God's love for us. God's grace working through that repentance saves us and changes the way we live.

The Scripture also says that salvation comes first; change is the result of salvation. Read the story of Zacchaeus in Luke 19:1-10. Zacchaeus was another tax collector, an outcast. Jesus went to his home for dinner. The people grumbled, "Look. He's eating and drinking with a sinner" (see 19:7). Jesus—read *salvation*—came to Zacchaeus's house; and Zacchaeus was changed. He returned the money he had stolen and gave still more to the poor. Salvation, for Zacchaeus, resulted in change. He was transformed.

The Bible offers a variety of ways to understand salvation. Some of them clearly support our belief that salvation is transformational. Being saved is being changed into a better or even a perfect person. Each of us is gathered into the waiting arms of Christ and changed.

So, Who Is Saved?

Another image of salvation is the presence of Christ in the community of sinners. What evidence do you see in the major arenas of your life (family, work, school, church, leisure) of Christ in "the community of sinners"?

So, Who Is Saved?

Read Matthew 9:9-13 again. Notice: There is no mention of repentance or transformation. Matthew was a tax collector. He went with Jesus to a dinner party where there were other tax collectors and sinners. Apparently they were unrepentant. They had not miraculously changed just because they were at dinner. They were changed because of who else was at that dinner. Jesus sat at table with persons who were invited to come just as they were. In his gracious presence, they were called to become more than they were; to experience the mercy of God through Jesus the Son.

By eating and drinking with outcasts, Jesus challenges the faith of the Pharisees. The Pharisees grumbled because they thought God was interested only in the righteous. Jesus said no; God calls to the lost as well as to the saved; the sinner as well as the righteous. By entertaining sinners, Jesus brought them into community. Salvation is the presence of Christ in the community of sinners.

What About Us?

Use all but the last paragraph of this section as a meditation. Read it slowly and take time to re-create and fill in the images of this scene in your mind.

What About Us?

Jesus invites us to be a part of the community. He opens the door wide and invites us in. Imagine. Walk down a city street at night. Gray buildings fade into gray sidewalks. The streets are wet with rain. Streetlights turn the clouds an eerie pink. No one's in the city at night. Businesses are closed. The theater crowd's gone home. You hear the clatter of your own footsteps. Up ahead, light from a window floods the sidewalk, like a porch light welcoming you home. You walk closer and peer in the window—your nose on the glass of an all-night restaurant.

Inside, a group of people sits at the tables. A woman sits drinking coffee, briefcase open, going over reports. Nearby, a couple who have apparently just left the theater treat themselves to a snack. A man with his son, still in his sports uniform, laugh over sundaes. Good; a safe place.

You go inside, only to see a man with a knit cap, his skin slick with rain and lined with dirt, shoveling in a plate of eggs. A woman makes a pass at him. An old man sips on a bottle in a brown paper bag. A teenager with Coke-bottle glasses plays cards; his companion lays a gun on the table. A man sits with one foot on the edge of the table, talking to a woman in black with a rose tattoo on her breast. A man in a blue tattered suit pulls up a chair. A waitress leans over a counter, watching. Do you go back out or stay there? Tell the ragtag bunch to leave? Sit only with the "nice" folks?

After the reading, consider these questions: How do you feel? Would you walk into the restaurant? Would you keep walking? Do you experience the open door as a comfort or a threat? Why? How do you feel that you can't close the door or control who comes in?

Jesus invites us to be part of a community in which "tax collectors and sinners" are also welcome. Among the saved are outcasts, people we don't much like. They scare us. We don't really want to hang out with the wrong crowd. But the door is open, and we can't close it. The radical love of Jesus won't let us shut out or put out anyone. And we, though we fall short as well, are always welcome.

What About the Church?

How is the story about Jesus' call of Matthew the story of the church?

What About the Church?

The Scripture creates a picture of salvation: Jesus sitting at a table with "tax collectors and sinners." It's also meant to be a picture of the church. If Jesus saves sinners, gathers them together in communities; then the church should do the same. If Jesus opens wide the doors of salvation, church doors should be wide open.

Make a guest list. Who would Jesus welcome into the church? Who would Jesus welcome into your church that you or others there might not want to

The problem, of course, is that some churches are busy shutting the doors. We may be tempted to set ourselves apart as a holy

come in? In what ways is their presence with you a mutual blessing? What are specific ways you can change your community of faith so that "tax collectors and sinners" feel welcome? If you are a "tax collector or sinner" what gifts do you bring to the community of faith and what gifts do you hope to receive?

Close With Prayer

Take time to review your insights from the session. What might God be calling you to do or to be as a result? What barriers might you be challenged to break down? Of what attitudes, behaviors, or beliefs are you being called to repent?

Take those discoveries to God in prayer, closing with "God, take away our confusion and lead us to your table, where sinners are saved through Jesus Christ. Amen."

people, somehow untouched by a sinful, secular world. We may establish committees to determine who's in and who's out and in so doing, exclude the people we don't like. Does the church today look like the Gospel's picture of a saved community?

If not, what happens next? We repent and change. We learn to be merciful, living in God's amazing grace. We open wide our doors and set a table for Jesus.

Jesus was a troublemaker. He ate and drank with outcasts. He spent his time with real sinners. By doing so, Jesus challenged our social structures, our self-perception, our ways of thinking about salvation. Being saved means being with Jesus and his friends, hanging out with people the world and the church despise. Jesus makes trouble because he threatens us: "I have come to call not the righteous but sinners." How do we see ourselves and others?

Session Three

Cleansing the Temple

It's the night before the annual church bazaar, soup supper, and antique auction—the big event of the year that makes about one-fourth of the annual budget. Right in the middle of frantic last-minute preparations, someone asks, "Didn't Jesus cleanse the Temple because of the moneychangers? I wonder what he'd think about us?" Now that's a great mood-killer!

Jesus didn't actually "cleanse" the Temple. To "cleanse" the Temple would have implied that it was somehow ritually impure and needed to be ritually cleansed. Jesus never suggested anything like that. He had a positive attitude toward and relationship with the Temple. What Jesus did do was to issue a prophetic challenge to abuses of the Temple system that exploited the poor and excluded them from the community at worship.

The Geography of the Temple

The geography of the Temple Mount is important for our story. The Temple Mount covered some thirty-five acres; the Temple itself was only a small part of the entire complex. The vast open area was known as the Court of the Gentiles and functioned as a public gathering place. It was a place of worship for the Gentiles, a public traffic-way through the Temple Mount, and a place of business. At the south end of the Temple Mount was a three-story building, known as

Session Focus

Jesus drove the moneychangers out of the Temple to protest injustice.

Session Objective

To see Jesus' action in the context of his concern for the poor and those forced out of their opportunity for religious observance.

Session Preparation

Display drawings of what the Temple looked like in Jesus' day. Many study Bibles have this diagram. Have on hand a Bible dictionary and a commentary on the Gospels.

Choose from among these activities and discussion starters to plan your lesson.

The Temple

Look carefully at the map of the Temple and any pictures that may be displayed. Find the location of the Royal Stoa. How would it be, do you think, if every time you came to church, you had to walk through an area that was as crowded, noisy, and commercial as an airport concourse or the mall just before Christmas?

the Royal Stoa. The Royal Stoa held the offices and vaults of the Temple treasury and the public treasury as well. It was a sort of "First National Bank of Jerusalem." Here we would find the tables of the moneychangers and the stalls of those who sold animals for the sacrifices. This was the area of the Temple Mount where Jesus staged his prophetic action.

Why Have Moneychangers?

Have you ever traveled to a country in which US currency was not taken? How did you obtain the proper currency? What was the exchange rate and what service fee did you pay for the conversion? If you changed money at the airport, and then at a hotel, and then elsewhere in the business or tourist areas, did you pay and receive exactly the same rates? Did you ever feel that you had been cheated or that your position as a newcomer left you vulnerable to exploitation? What could you do about it?

What was the process for pilgrims traveling to Jerusalem for the Passover? What options did the pilgrims have?

Why Have Moneychangers and Stock Sellers at All?

The moneychangers and stock sellers were performing an important public service. Each male Jew was required to pay a Temple tax each year, and this tax could not be paid in the coins commonly circulating in the marketplace. Those coins carried portraits of the emperor, or of the pagan gods, and were therefore violations of the commandments against idolatry and graven images. So ordinary money had to be exchanged for Tyrian shekels, which did not carry forbidden images.

No one would argue that moneychangers were not entitled to a fee for services, just as we pay a fee when we purchase traveler's checks, or change dollars to pounds or yen. But, there was no regulation of the moneychangers and no fees set by government control. Can you see the potential for abuse?

In practice, the fee for service was often as much as 100 to 150 percent of the amount of money changed. This was a great hardship for the poor, who often earned only a few shekels a year and had already paid out several frontier taxes (to people like Matthew and Zacchaeus) on their way to Jerusalem. Jesus' action would have been enthusiastically supported by the poor, who often arrived in Jerusalem angry and without money. Imagine if you had to pay a service charge of $125 in order to purchase $100 worth of traveler's checks!

What were the good reasons for having moneychangers and stock sellers in the Temple? How were they a help to worshipers? What was the potential for exploitation? Spell out that potential in detail. How would you work it, if you were in charge? What did Jesus say was the business of the Temple?

The stock sellers also performed a valuable and needed service. Animals offered as sacrifices in the Temple proper had to be without spot or blemish. In theory, one could bring a sacrificial animal from home; but trying to bring an animal the long distance from Galilee, not to mention Babylon or Rome, just wasn't practical.

There was an added difficulty in transporting an animal since it also had to be fed and quartered along the way. If a pilgrim brought his animal all that way and the priests declared it unfit for the sacrifice, the traveler had incurred great expense and inconvenience for nothing; far easier just to buy the animal in the Temple itself. But the stock sellers were also an unregulated monopoly, and there was the same potential for abuse that we have already seen with the moneychangers. Imagine how you'd feel if you had a perfectly good animal rejected, and then had to buy another animal at three times the price!

Given the potential for abuse in the system, then, one can argue that Jesus was protesting against the business environment of the Royal Portico. The heart of his protest was that business was not the business of the Temple. God had intended the Temple for worship and not for business. The fact that business interfered with worship by the Gentiles only made the practice worse.

How do fund-raisers fit into the "business" of the church? How does your church define its "business"?

Reconsider the introductory comments about the church bazaar. What is the business of the church? And how does the bazaar, or other fund-raising activities, fit into the business of the church?

John 2:13-22

John's setting for the "cleansing" is different from that found in the Synoptic Gospels. Matthew, Mark, and Luke set the event at the beginning of the last week of Jesus' life and suggest that it was the event that led the Temple authorities to decide to do away with Jesus. It is unlikely that Jesus performed this prophetic action twice, so the four Gospels probably record the same event.

Why, then, does John have the "cleansing" at the beginning of Jesus' ministry, rather than at the end? There is an important theological reason for the change. For John's Gospel, Jesus is the source of grace and glory and the one who brings abundant new life to those who believe in him. John 1 and the first part of chapter 2 are about that grace and new life. In John 2:13-22, John points out that new life brings a challenge to the existing order. If one accepts Jesus' glory and grace and begins to live in the new life, one can no longer accept the status quo, but must challenge it in God's name.

This is what Jesus himself did, when he challenged the abuses of the mercantile system in the Temple. He made a whip of cords (only John has this detail) and drove the animals out of the Temple. He "poured out the coins of the money changers" (2:15). In the Greek, verses 14-16 are one long sentence, suggesting a sort of breathless haste about getting through the story: animals, customers, stock sellers, moneychangers, coins scattered and chaos all over. Imagine the disaster for record-keeping, not to mention the coins that mysteriously disappeared into the pockets of the crowd. Even if all the coins were recovered, who would ever know which coins belonged to whom?

On one level, Jesus' prophetic action can

John 2:13-22 ■

Read John 2:13-22. Try to recreate the scene. To do this, retell and augment the story with "color." One person will start by describing the surroundings. In turns, add dimensions to the story from what the Scripture tells you and from what you imagine the scene to be like, based on what you know about the Temple precincts, about animals and what happens when they eat, and about crowd behavior.

Bible 301 □

Review this passage in a commentary, such as The New Interpreter's Bible, *Volume VIII (Abingdon, 1995) to get a more complete picture of the Temple setup regarding the animal stalls, moneychangers, and so on. What is the theological reason why John has this narrative at the beginning of his Gospel?*

What did Jesus really do? John adds the detail that Jesus made a whip of cords and used it to drive certain people out of the Temple. What does it mean to you that Jesus resorted to this physical, perhaps violent, display to make his point? Given that it only disrupted business briefly, why, do you think, did he bother?

How did Jesus challenge these Temple practices and the system? How did the Temple authorities react to his challenge?

Imagine that Jesus came to your church bazaar and auction (mentioned at the beginning of the chapter) and started turning over tables and driving off the auctioneer and booth owners. Would you just be angry and stunned (or something else), or would you feel challenged to re-evaluate your purposes for holding the event?

be seen as a social and economic protest on behalf of the poor, just as in the Synoptic Gospels. He attacked the abuses of a system that fell hardest on the poor. In doing so, he stands in the great tradition of prophets like Amos, Hosea, Isaiah, Micah, and Jeremiah—those who called for economic and social justice for the poor.

On another level, Jesus' prophetic action challenges the religious system itself. Jesus says to those who were selling the doves, "Stop making my Father's house a marketplace!" (2:16). Since the marketplace was a key part of the system of sacrifice and tithes, Jesus' challenge was far more radical than just a protest against economic abuses. He challenged the very authority of the Temple itself.

A House of Prayer

Read Isaiah 56:1-12 to get an idea of the vision of a restored Jerusalem. How did Jesus use his knowledge of this Scripture in his indictment of the Temple practice he condemned? Whose cause was he championing and what effect do you think it was intended to have?

A House of Prayer for All Nations

Jesus quoted from Isaiah 56:7 and Jeremiah 7:11 in questioning whether the Temple, which was to be a place of prayer for all the nations, was in effect a den of robbers.

Isaiah offered a vision of a restored Jerusalem and a renewed Temple that would serve not only as a center of worship for the returned exiles, but as a place of prayer for all the nations. Jesus compared the current travesty in the Court of the Gentiles with the faithless behavior of his forebears and held up the vision of the new Temple as the ideal toward which all his countrymen should have been working.

By using the Court of the Gentiles, the only place of worship available to "all the nations," as a place to serve a flood of visitors, the Temple authorities had either shut down or severely curtailed the worship opportunities for the Gentile pilgrims to the Passover.

A Day of Chaos

What kind of "chaos" do we need to be creating in our churches? As faithful Christians, should we be calling our leaders' attention to some church practices that do not further the church's mission?

A Day of Chaos

Jesus' disruption created chaos in the Court of the Gentiles and put to an end (at least for the day) the payment of the Temple tax and the offering of sacrifices (at least those dependent on the sale of animals in the Temple). This disruption of the Temple system happened during Passover, the busiest and most important season of the year that saw perhaps one hundred thousand pilgrims flooding into the city and Temple precincts. Imagine the chaos if someone were to shut down all the computers and cash registers in all the shopping malls of a major city just six days before Christmas! On a somewhat smaller scale, that's what Jesus accomplished that morning in the Temple. It's no wonder that the religious leaders asked him by what authority he did this.

We need to remember that Jesus was not opposed to the Temple itself. Nor was he opposed to Jewish tradition, faith, or way of life. Jesus was a practicing Jew, who worshiped regularly in the Temple. In fact, John's Gospel has Jesus in the Temple at all the major feasts on the Jewish calendar. Rather, it was as a faithful Jew, one who held the Temple in high regard, that Jesus entered his protest. His challenge was not to Temple worship, but to a religious system that was so deeply entrenched it could not see what God was doing. It was no longer open to a fresh revelation from God.

A Continuing Challenge

How was Jesus' action a protest on behalf of the poor? How did his action challenge the religious system? What do we do with

A Continuing Challenge

The followers of Jesus continue to face enormous economic challenges to the poor. Economic statistics consistently repeat that the gap between the haves and have-nots is growing in the United States. It is growing

the challenge Jesus sets before us? Is justice really that important?

even faster between the United States and countries in Africa and southern Asia, which leads to a hard question for us.

As we accept Jesus' grace and glory and proclaim him as Son of God, what do we do with the challenges he sets before us? Does being a faithful follower of Jesus mean we need to deal with economic inequity? What would economic justice look like for Africa, given that the planet does not have enough resources to raise their standard of living to a level equal with ours?

After the Outburst

Read Psalm 69. What is the psalmist's lament and prayer? What seems to be his situation, and how does he feel about it? What case does he make before God, and what does he ask of God?

How has the psalmist's zeal served him and what has been the consequence? What about this psalm would have brought it to the minds of the disciples? In what new light might they have seen Jesus and his actions?

How does the tense change in *consume* affect the Temple story and what Jesus was saying and doing?

After the Outburst

Following Jesus' passionate outburst against the moneychangers, the disciples remembered Psalm 69:9 (because the writer wanted his readers to see Jesus' action through the lens of that psalm). The Gospel writer also made a minor, but theologically crucial change, in the wording of the psalm: "Zeal for your house will consume me" (John 2:17). In the original psalm, "It is zeal for your house that has consumed me," the verb *consume* is in the past tense, not future tense. This changes the meaning from something that has happened in the past to a prophecy of Jesus being consumed (crucified).

This reminds us that John's Temple story is not about the Temple so much as it is about Jesus. The way the story is written forces us to ask questions about who Jesus is and the authority by which he acts. What happens if we take seriously the questions about Jesus and Jesus' authority? If Jesus is truly God's Son, God's own presence in the world (as we say he is, every time we repeat the creeds), then does that give an added importance to his calls for justice for the poor? for challenging entrenched systems?

By What Authority?

The religious authorities (John 2:18) asked Jesus for a "sign," that is, for some credentials that gave him the authority to upset the Temple system. Just who do you think you are, Jesus? Jesus responded with a saying about the destruction of the Temple, which the authorities didn't understand. The Temple at this time had been under construction for forty-six years; how could Jesus rebuild it in three days?

Actually, work on the Temple proper was completed quickly. However, construction continued on other parts of the Temple Mount until well past the time of Jesus. In fact, when work on the Temple was finally completed, around A.D. 60, so many workmen were suddenly unemployed that there was an economic crisis. King Herod Agrippa put them to work building new streets in Jerusalem. The king took responsibility for seeing that workmen who depended on a daily wage were not thrown out of work—the very thing the prophets and psalmists said he was supposed to do.

Jesus replied that, if the Temple were destroyed, he would "raise it up" in three days. "Raise it up" is also used to refer to "resurrection." So we already have a deeper insight as to what Jesus was talking about.

The Temple authorities, most of whom would have been Sadducees, did not believe in resurrection and would have been offended both by the notion that Jesus could miraculously rebuild the Temple and by the notion that Jesus would be raised from death. The writer goes on, in verse 21, to make the implicit deeper meaning plain. He explains to his readers exactly what is going on. The Temple is replaced by Jesus' body in this saying. Since the Temple was considered by

By What Authority?

Review John 2:18-22. What is the debate with the authorities about? What do they want, and how did Jesus answer them?

Imagine again that Jesus has disrupted your bazaar and that the pastor and chairpersons of the finance and worship committees have accosted him about what authority he had to do such a thing. What kind of answer do you think Jesus might make?

What would it take for you to consider his reason authoritative enough for you to change or to reconsider what you were doing?

Bible 301

Look up Saddducees *in a Bible dictionary. Pay particular attention to their beliefs, including those about resurrection. How would Jesus' comments about being raised up affect the Sadducees? How would they have affected the theological tensions between the Sadducees and the Pharisees?*

faithful Jews as the place where God was present on earth, so the deeper meaning also suggests that Jesus' body had become that place.

Matthew 21:12-17

Make a parallel comparison of this episode in all four Gospels (Matthew 21:12-17, Mark 11:15-19, Luke 19:45-48, John 2:13-22). What is the same in all four accounts? What is different about Matthew's account of the action in the Temple? What do you think the differences mean?

Matthew 21:12-17

Matthew gives no indication that he was aware of any abuse in the practice of changing coins and selling sacrificial animals in the Temple. (Matthew's Gospel is more concerned with theological understandings than with social justice issues.) But by the time the Gospels were written, the Temple was no longer standing, and any social justice issues connected with it had long become moot. Matthew's concern, given the destruction of the Temple, was where do the people of God go from here? What is the new symbol of God's presence among God's people? How does Matthew answer these questions?

First, following Mark, he has Jesus "driving out" the buyers and sellers and overturning the tables of the moneychangers (Mark 11:15-19). He kept Jesus' saying about the house of prayer and the den of robbers (Mark 11:17; Matthew 21:13), a combination of Isaiah 56:7 and Jeremiah 7:11.

Read Jeremiah 7:1-15. What was the nature of Jeremiah's polemic? To whom was Jeremiah speaking and what was their situation? What excuses were the religious leaders offering for their behavior that Jeremiah condemned? How does this passage fit the message that Jesus conveyed to his hearers?

The "den of robbers" refers to the background of the Jeremiah text. Jeremiah preached to a people on the brink of captivity and exile who believed the Temple was a guarantee of divine protection. He said they treated the Temple like a robber's hideout where they could hide after acts of injustice (Jeremiah 7:1-11). That is, those whose control of political and economic power structures made it possible for them to exploit the poor who then claimed the Temple as God's dwelling and their own personal place of prayer. Jeremiah referred to these exploiters of the poor with the proper term—thieves—

and said they were abusing the Temple by using it as a hideout for thieves. Jesus said the social-religious-economic system was abusing the Temple by turning it into a marketplace. Both Jeremiah and Jesus condemned the use of the Temple to "cover" acts of injustice against the poor and marginalized.

Reclaiming the Temple

Jesus seemed to emphasize welcoming the neglected and excluded. Who were they? Why was it important to welcome them? Who are the neglected and excluded in our day? That is, in practice, whom do we not welcome in the church? What would Jesus say to us about including them in the community?

Reclaiming the Temple

Second, Matthew understood that Jesus not only cast out those who used the Temple as a hideout instead of a place of prayer, he welcomed those who were neglected and excluded—the blind, the lame, the children. The blind and lame came to him in the Temple and were cured. Jesus not only healed them physically; the act of healing also restored them to full membership in the community.

In the complicated social and religious system of Jesus' day, those whose bodies bore some kind of imperfection were often considered "unclean" and were not allowed to be full members of the community. The act of healing them physically, then, also made it possible for them to take a place in the worshiping community again.

Sing or read together "All Glory, Laud, and Honor," which refers to the Hosannas sung by the children and to the role of Jesus as the son of David. Imagine the excitement behind the original song. What sort of expectations would that original event have carried? How does the hymn transcend time to help you feel a part of that original event and anticipation? Why would this acclamation have elicited a fearful response from anyone?

Children in the first century were not treated in the same way we treat children. They were marginalized, often treated as property, often hungry and ragged, and had few or no rights in the community. It is these marginalized ones who proclaim Jesus as "Son of David," or "Messiah." It is interesting to note that David was a man of action, even of violence; and many in Israel expected the Messiah to bring God's violent judgment of God's enemies. Instead, the violence comes on the religious system of Israel itself. To some extent, at least, Jesus' action in the

Temple was a violent sign of judgment on those who rob the poor in the name of religion and who exclude any of God's "children" (including the Gentiles) from the community of faith.

Bible 301: The Son of David

Look up Son of David *in a Bible dictionary. How would Jesus' association with David have been viewed as good news by some and a threat by others?*

The Son of David

Third, Jesus accepted the title "Son of David." The Jewish authorities, therefore, were greatly concerned about what the children were saying (Matthew 21:15). "Hosanna to the son of David" elicited fear less in terms of prophetic action than that someone was claiming to be Messiah, to be acting with the authority and power of God. The claim to be Messiah, in itself, caused trouble. The Roman rulers of Judea would not allow anyone who claimed to be a rightful local ruler to live very long. So the Jewish authorities were concerned that word not get around that Jesus could be considered a claimant to Herod's throne. They preferred to keep the peace, which meant keeping the Romans happy. Jesus "shook up" the system in almost everything he did and said!

Temple to Church

Where is the presence of the Son of David most obvious and efficacious for you? What evidence to you see of the work of Christ in your church and elsewhere in your life?

Have you ever felt pushed out or excluded from the community of faith? Have you ever been tempted to push out or deny someone else? Take a few minutes to write in a journal or to talk to one other person about that experience. What was

Temple to Church

The first Temple had been built by King Solomon, David's son and heir. But David had collected the materials and amassed the wealth that made the building of the Temple possible. It was in this Temple that God's presence among the people was made known. When Jesus was acknowledged as the Son of David, he began to build the foundation for the church—a community of faith—in which God's presence is made known. The presence of God in the church is recognized and praised by the "little ones," those who are on the outside of established religious community structures. Both Jesus during his

it like? What did you do? How did you experience God in that situation? In what ways, if any, do you feel that it transformed or challenged you?

ministry and Jesus' followers in the church opened the doors of the community to those who had previously been excluded. Throughout history, whenever the church has been most faithful to its Master, it has welcomed the poor, the hungry, the outcast, those whom society pushes to the margins and treats as second-class.

What About Us?

Does God still call us to do the same kinds of things Jesus was doing? What would that mean in our day? Is economic and social justice really that important? What about "unclean" persons? Is our church, our community of faith, one in which God's presence is made known? Do the "little ones" praise God in our congregation? Or are they excluded, or at least told to be quiet? (Remember that "little ones" means more than children.)

Close With Devotions

Review the radical actions of Jesus from this session, and evaluate how his courage lays a claim on your heart and mind. What attitudes and behaviors are challenged? Include these assessments in prayer, or conclude with a petition that God will forgive us when we become too much like the moneychangers in the Temple and not enough like Jesus, who acted on behalf of the poor and the excluded.

What About Us?

What do Matthew and John's reports about Jesus cleansing the Temple have to teach us about our day? There are as many questions as answers. What new thing is God doing in our day? How do we recognize what God is doing?

One clue to an answer is that God continues to do the same kinds of things Jesus was doing in Jerusalem—and God calls the church to the same ministries. That is, God calls for social and economic justice for the poor, for those who are shoved aside by the majority culture and "left out" of the economic miracle of our decade. God calls us to include in the life of the community the people that we would rather not include. In Jesus' day, that group included persons considered ritually "unclean." We often identify as "unclean" persons such as gay men and lesbians, the homeless and hungry, persons on welfare, and so on. Children were often excluded from the community in Jesus' day. In spite of the rhetoric about education in public debate, children in the United States are often left on the margins of society, particularly those in inner cities, in pockets of poverty in rural locales, on reservations. Jesus opened up the community (much to the dismay of that community, at times) to those who were marginalized and unclean. Does God expect any less of us?

Session Four

Jesus Challenges the Interpretation of Scripture

Session Focus

Jesus challenged the current reigning interpretations of Scripture and sometimes, Scripture itself.

Session Objective

To discover and practice Jesus' model of interpreting Scripture.

Session Preparation

Read the chapter carefully. Be sure you understand the "drill down" method well enough to explain it.

Have on hand hymnals and a Bible dictionary.

Choose from among these activities and discussion starters to plan your lesson.

The Bible Says . . .

How do we understand Scripture? What is its authority? On what issues have we decided that what Scripture says no longer applies? Why did we decide that? What other issues still

The Bible Says . . .

One of the major issues for American Protestantism is how we interpret Scripture. What is the authority of Scripture? How do we use it? At least one major denomination, citing the authority of Scripture, has denied women the right to serve as pastors in the church. United Methodists and United Presbyterians are anything but united when it comes to the question of homosexuality. Honest and thoughtful Christians on both sides of that divide appeal to Scripture as the authority for their position. On other issues, such as divorce, slavery, dietary laws, and so on, American Protestants selectively apply and recognize the authority of Scripture, ignoring what seems culturally outmoded. We often hear, "But if we don't believe a part of the Bible, how can we believe any of it?" All of these questions are difficult and incredibly important.

Without getting into specific details on any of the thorny issues mentioned above (and dozens of others), what can we learn from the way Jesus dealt with Scripture? It's clear that, in his ministry, Jesus challenged the current reigning interpretations of Scripture, and, sometimes, Scripture itself. In this chapter, we will look at Jesus' challenges,

remain, on which we have not made that judgment? How will we resolve them?

what lay behind them, and what we can learn from him about interpretation and authority. As we begin, we need to remember that, when the New Testament talks about Scripture, it means Hebrew Scripture. The Torah (Law) and the Prophets (which, for Judaism includes the books we call "history") were considered Scripture by the Jewish community in which Jesus and the early church lived. The Psalms were often cited as Scripture, but the status of the rest of the "Writings" (such as Chronicles, Ezra-Nehemiah, Proverbs, Daniel, and others) was not clear.

How Jesus Looked at Scripture

Read Matthew 5:17-20. We sometimes think that Jesus broke the law (though he didn't). What does this passage tell you about Jesus' approach to the law?

What does it mean to say that Jesus had a high view of the authority of Scripture? What is your view of the authority of Scripture?

How Jesus Looked at Scripture

We begin by noting that Jesus took the authority of Scripture seriously. Matthew 5:17-20 (see Luke 16:17) is a saying that Matthew took from *Q* (the sayings source used by both Matthew and Luke) and rewrote to introduce Jesus' challenges to the interpretation of Scripture. Two points are important here.

First, Jesus has a high view of the authority of Scripture. Not even the stroke of a letter will pass away, and whoever breaks even the least of the commandments is not barred from the Kingdom but is among the least in it. We need to be clear: "till heaven and earth pass away" does not mean the same thing as "always and forever," but until the Kingdom comes.

The Torah has a continuing validity, but it is not the ultimate authority. The Kingdom has now come, and the word of Jesus is the ultimate revelation of God. So a new authority now takes the place of Scripture. Scripture is affirmed; but it is also put in a role of secondary importance, relative to the word of Jesus.

Second, Jesus came to "fulfill" the law and the prophets. And yet Jesus himself lived in a considerable freedom from both the written Torah and the oral traditions that interpreted Torah. So there were questions among his hearers: Is Torah still valid? Has the Torah been abolished by the coming of the Kingdom? We are still struggling with that question today. Who has not heard the comment, "Jesus did away with the old law, and we're free from all that."

What does Matthew mean when he says that Jesus fulfilled the Scripture? Is that what we usually mean when we say that? What's the difference? What new insights into Scripture does Matthew give us, about which we need to think some more?

Changes in the Early Church

The community for which Matthew wrote (around A.D. 80–100) made fundamental changes in the way it interpreted and practiced Torah. Because of this, they were under attack from the Jewish community. So Matthew was trying to answer the charges of being unfaithful to Torah, on the one hand and, on the other, to help his community to a clearer understanding of the relationship between being obedient to the Torah and being a faithful disciple of Jesus.

So, Matthew says, Jesus did not abolish the Torah, but neither did he affirm all the status quo of the way the faith community should interpret and practice Torah. He came to "fulfill the Scripture." What does that mean for Matthew?

- All of Scripture testifies to God's will and work in history. For Matthew, the ceremonial laws are not less important than the moral laws (as opposed to what later Christians have often said).
- God's work is not yet complete. The Torah and Prophets point beyond themselves to God's definitive act in Jesus Christ.
- The coming of the Kingdom is the fulfillment of the Torah.

Changes in the Church

The early Jewish Christians lived in a religious "both / and" of accepting Christ as Savior, but living out that belief in the context of Hebrew tradition and Jewish culture. Have you ever been "between cultures"? felt as if you had to justify your beliefs?

Review the five comments on "fulfilling Scripture." These comments note that there is a Kingdom dimension in this fulfillment and that fulfilling Scripture encompasses all of Scripture. How does taking a broad, rather than a narrow, view change the practical aspects of what you do based on your view? How do we respect the authority, validity, and efficacy of the Hebrew Scriptures (which are a valuable portion of our own Scriptures) if we say that Jesus transcended them?

When you consider the meaning and application of Scripture, are you thinking "locally" (that is, how does this affect my life today) or "universally" (that is, in light of what it means for God's kingdom)? What difference might that distinction make?

- The Kingdom does not make the Torah and Prophets obsolete, but confirms them.
- Confirmation is not the same as continuation or repetition of the original law. Fulfillment can also mean that the original teaching has been transcended. Jesus' statement that his own life and teaching are the definitive revelation of God's will (see Matthew 11:25-27; 28:18-20) means that neither the written Torah nor the oral tradition is the final authority. Jesus, and Jesus alone, is the final authority on the will of God.

Some Characteristics

Skim through Matthew 5:21-48 to get a sense of it. (You will examine it more closely in smaller segments.) Keep in mind the structure of Jesus' observations: "You have heard . . . but I say to you."

Some Characteristics of Jesus' Challenge

In Matthew 5:21-48, we find a series of anti-theses to teachings in both the Torah and the oral tradition. Jesus challenged both text and interpretation and said the ultimate authority is not in the written text, but in himself. His teaching does not transgress the Scripture, but transcends it.

How does that work? If the Sermon on the Mount were a web site, and you were to click on *murder*, the computer would bring up a list of words and options that you could explore further. Clicking on *causes for murder*, would lead to another menu that might include anger, scorn, and so on. Clicking on *anger* might then lead to another menu that could have the question "How do I apply this teaching to my life?" Jesus did the same thing with words—he "drilled down" through the Torah in three steps.

What is the "drill-down" method of challenging / interpreting Scripture? What are the three steps? How did Jesus use it? Does that model make sense for the way Jesus taught?

Note: Take time to learn how to distinguish these three steps. You will be asked to practice them with Matthew 5:21-48.

1. Jesus reaffirmed the Torah. ("It was said to those of ancient times . . .")

2. Jesus radicalized the teaching of the Torah. ("But I say to you . . .") This is not a denial of the Torah, but a "drill down" to the heart of the meaning of Torah. The ancient

Read Matthew 5:21-26. What are the surface issues? What "radicalization" or deeper issue is at the heart of this teaching?

What ways do we have of discerning what God's perfect or absolute will is for us? As flawed beings, can we ever live out or live up to an absolute? If absolutes are impossible to keep, is there a point in establishing them? (Of course, if they are established by God, the point is God's, not ours, to decide.)

Using reconciliation as the issue, think about times when you "came to the altar," carrying a load of anger or resentment. How did you deal with it? Though this passage is more about reconciliation than about worship, what benefit, if any, do you find in bringing your anger and resentment "to the altar"?

teaching is an important clue to God's will, but does not go to the heart of it. The heart of the meaning is much closer to what Jesus stated.

3. Finally, Jesus gave a creative model for how imperfect people who fall short of doing the perfect will of God can still live with the radical teaching.

For example, take the ethical demands around murder. Jesus affirmed the teaching against murder (don't do it!), and then radicalized the teaching. It is God's will, not only that we not commit murder but that we not even be angry with our brother or sister. Obviously, this is an impossible demand for human beings—in fact, Jesus himself was angry on more than one occasion.

But since Jesus declared the demand to be the absolute will of God, there must be some creative model of behavior that allows imperfect persons to live out God's will. In this case, the model is that the disciples are called to work for reconciliation—overcoming alienation and hostility, rather than concentrating on ritual—because of their expectation of the Kingdom that Jesus had inaugurated.

(Note: Jesus probably didn't mean literally that the disciples should get up and walk out of the worship service to go reconcile with the neighbor.) Reconciliation is the absolute will of God where there is anger and estrangement. And here's the key: the disciples (we) are responsible for finding ways to use creatively what Jesus says about living out God's will in a less-than-perfect world. Jesus did not give us a legal formula for dealing with less-than-perfect behavior; that's a worthless approach. Jesus calls us, instead, to recognize the realities in our lives compared to God's will and to figure out how to move toward living out God's will.

More Drill-Down Models

The Sermon on the Mount presents Jesus spelling out what a radical "drill-down" means and how disciples could live that out. In each case, he follows the same pattern.

Adultery. Jesus reaffirmed the commandment against adultery (Matthew 5:27-30), but then "drilled down." The real issue is lust; it is the intention of the heart that makes one guilty before God. Radical sin, Jesus said, calls for radical measures; hence the hyperbole about gouging out the eye and severing limbs.

Note the problems if we take verse 29 literally. First, there would be an awful lot of blind and dismembered people on our streets! Second, that would not solve the problem of lust, which can continue to function perfectly well without eyesight or hands. So what's the solution? Jesus would have recognized that we do not always measure up to absolute standards, but that lapses must be resisted with radical measures. Each disciple must look within at the intention as well as the act and work toward realigning him- or herself with God's will.

Marriage. The second example deals with love in marriage, or, perhaps more accurately, the loss of love in marriage (5:31-32). Divorce and remarriage were acceptable to Torah (the Scripture of Jesus' day) and regulated by it, just as they are acceptable in our society and regulated by law and custom (see Deuteronomy 24:1-4). In Jewish culture, divorce was weighted in favor of the male—women apparently had few, if any, rights of divorce. Jesus, however, said that divorce and remarriage are a violation of the seventh

More Drill-Down Models ■

Form five small groups to investigate the other five examples of Jesus' ethical teachings.

Bible 301 □

Use a Bible commentary, such as The New Interpreter's Bible, *Volume VIII (Abingdon Press, 1995) to gain a greater insight into each of these passages.*

Adultery ■

Read Matthew 5:27-30. What are the problems if we take Jesus' teachings on adultery literally? If the intention of the heart matters first (as well as our behavior), how can we ever feel free from judgment? Can we control what we feel or even what we think? What is the core issue here? How do we apply this teaching to our own lives?

Marriage ■

Read Matthew 5:31-32. How does Jesus radicalize the teaching about marriage and divorce? What options does that leave? What is the deeper issue?

On a practical level in a nation with a very high divorce rate, is the charge anything other than an ancient or quaint novelty? How might our relationships be stronger or better if we radicalized this teaching? How do we apply this teaching to our own relationships?

commandment (though there is an "exception clause").

Jesus radicalized the understanding of marriage. He said it is not something contractual, to be regulated by society. It is a gift from God, not something at human disposal. So the radical demand is to live out God's will for life-long, monogamous relationships. This radical demand takes us beyond what we often find in our society—a kind of "five-year contract, with an option to renew" approach to marriage. But, if marriage becomes destructive of persons, Christian disciples are called to struggle creatively with the tension between God's perfect will and their own weaknesses. There are no easy rules to follow. We have to struggle with the question of what it means to love in a situation like this.

Oath-taking ■

Read Matthew 5:33-37. What is the presenting issue? the core issue?

Is lying always wrong? If not, how do we reconcile the commands to take no oaths and to bear no false witness when to follow would advance a greater evil? How do we apply this command to life today?

Oath-taking. Jesus affirmed the old scriptural commandment about keeping one's oath (5:33-37). An oath confirmed that something was true, just what oaths taken in our courts are supposed to do. Jesus "drilled down" to the real issue: telling the truth. Don't, he says, take oaths at all.

The radicalization of the command is that oaths should not be necessary, since there is an absolute demand that all words are to be true for his disciples. Now, we all recognize situations in which the most loving, Christian, thing to do would be to lie. For example, families in Europe who were sheltering Jews often lied when asked by the Nazis about the presence of Jews. In that situation, it seemed the most loving thing to do, even though a literal following of Jesus' words could have meant telling the Nazis where the Jews were hidden. When Christian disciples come crashing against the limitations of the world's reality, they have to struggle to find creative solutions to the tension created when two demands of God's perfect will seem to clash.

Retaliation

Read Matthew 5:38-42 and Genesis 4:23-24. How have you typically interpreted the injunction, "an eye for an eye"? What is the deeper issue here? How does using a principle of proportionality serve the interests of justice and fairness?

Retaliation. "I don't get mad; I get even." Have you heard that, or something like it, recently? The Torah sought to curb revenge by means of the law of retaliation. Torah moved from the case of Lamech murdering a person who struck him (Genesis 4:23-24) to the principle of exact punishment, "an eye for an eye."

Jesus "drilled down" beneath this argument (and arguments in favor of capital punishment) to reject the principle of retaliatory violence (Matthew 5:38-42). Retaliation and violence are evil and not a part of the kingdom of God. The saying about violence is about a clash of kingdoms. To which kingdom do we give ultimate loyalty? Evil is real, but not ultimate. Love is both real and ultimate. To which do we give ultimate loyalty? Jesus says to take positive action to overcome violence and evil. Jesus did not advocate passive resistance, but positive action.

Look at each of the other commands here: turn the cheek, give your cloak, go the second mile, give to one who begs, and lend to a borrower. What is the deeper issue in each case? How are we called to live out these injunctions today?

All five examples of how one might respond are about an aggressive pressure from others who violate one's personal freedom and interest. All are radical responses. Offering the other cheek, for example, was (in Jesus' culture) offering to accept a deadly insult, rather than retaliate (5:39). "Going the second mile" was not about a little extra effort, but a response to the demands of a soldier in an army of occupation (5:41). All five responses are examples of how one considers the good and the needs of the other and not one's own rights. So how would a Christian stand up for his or her rights? Jesus calls us to seek creative solutions to the violence and anger and oppression of our world.

Love Your Enemy

Read Matthew 5:43-48. This may be the most difficult command of all. What is the heart of this issue? What is the reason given for this generous love and what does it mean to you?

The last verse of this command (verse 48) really applies to all that Jesus had said. What does "perfection" mean in this context? How can we will what God wills and desire what God desires?

Bring the small groups together. How does this drill-down method help you get beyond literalism to a creative struggle with the real issues? How do the examples in the book help you see the importance of struggling to live out God's perfect will in a less-than-perfect world? Does "creative problem solving" make us more faithful or less faithful as disciples? Why?

The Lord of the Sabbath

Read Matthew 12:1-14 and the supporting Scriptures in this section of the main text.

Why is sabbath-keeping so important for the people of God? If we take the commandment on sabbath-

Love your enemy. Finally, Jesus calls us to love our enemies. Scripture said, "Love your neighbor and hate your enemy." Jesus "drilled down" beyond that to say that everyone is our neighbor, for all are children of the same Father, who sends rain on the righteous and the unrighteous. Anyone can love the neighbor, the one who loves us. What's the power in that? The radical response is to take the hard road and love the enemy, to pray for those who abuse and violate our rights. This is the context in which we are called to be perfect, as God is perfect, meaning to love those who continue to hurt us, just as God continues to love those who break the heart of God. There is no specific, clear-cut, legalistic way of going about that. We are simply called to love as God loves and find creative ways to live that out in our daily lives.

The Lord of the Sabbath

Keeping the sabbath is a distinctive mark of the people of God. Keeping the sabbath is a part of the Decalogue (Exodus 20:1-19); it was observed and blessed by God in creation (Genesis 2:1-3). So why did Jesus insist on violating the sabbath? Human good takes precedence over laws that concern God's honor. No rabbi in Jesus' day would have argued the priority of doing good on the sabbath. The issue was how to apply the principle.

Matthew 12:1-14 reflects Jesus' attitude toward the sabbath and his participation in the debate. In this situation, the disciples were hungry. Torah said they could legally pluck grain that did not belong to them

(Deuteronomy 23: 25). The question was, Could they do so on the sabbath? The Pharisees said no, on the grounds of God's honor.

In response, Jesus "drilled down" to the real will of God in the sabbath commandment, namely mercy toward the poor and hungry. The reference to David reflects the real intent of sabbath laws. David, on the basis of human need, could overrule ritual law and violate the sanctity of the house of God. How much more could Jesus, on the basis of human need, apply the deeper teaching of the sabbath law?

Jewish scholarship says that a point of law (*Halakah*) could not be established on the basis of a story (*Hagadah*), but required a clear statement of principle from the Torah. Matthew adds to Jesus' argument an example from the Law and the Prophets. Priests sacrifice on the sabbath, and that preparation is work (Numbers 28:9-10), so sacrifice is clearly more important than the sabbath. But, Jesus added, mercy is even greater than sacrifice (Hosea 6:6). Therefore, mercy is greater than the sabbath.

This little story gives us a glimpse of Jesus at work, arguing with the Pharisees on the basis of sound rabbinic principles. It also helps us see some of the struggles of the community for whom Matthew wrote. They clearly were interpreting Scripture in a way different from the standard interpretation of the synagogues, and Matthew was trying to show the validity of their interpretation.

This brings us to the real issue. The Son of Man (Jesus) is Lord of the sabbath. Christians know this, and others do not. The key to the argument is really not humanitarianism versus legalism, but the person of Jesus. This is the ultimate "drill-down." Jesus

keeping literally, what problems does that cause for us in our culture? How would we solve the problem of doing good and still keeping the sabbath? What did Jesus say about that issue? What do you think Jesus might say to us about keeping the sabbath?

Use the "drill-down" model to take another look at the issues surrounding sabbath-keeping in our culture.

Use hymnody to consider the purpose and importance of gathering for worship. Sing or read together a hymn or call to worship, such as "God Is Here" or "Jesus, We Want to Meet."

What is the value of worship and sabbath-keeping for you?

What does it mean to you that Jesus is Lord of the sabbath?

takes priority over the sabbath. One logical corollary of that statement for us is that Jesus' teachings and example take priority over other teachings in Scripture.

Tradition Versus Scripture

What is the point of the argument in Mark 7:1-23? How did Jesus "drill-down" to deal with it?

Review the three reasons Jesus gave about the interpretations of the elders. What is the difference between the spirit and the letter of the law in these examples? What did Jesus have to say about it?

What are some contemporary examples of following the letter of the law that either flaunts the spirit of the law or disregards a need that morally should take precedence?

Tradition Versus Scripture

Mark 7:1-23 is an extended argument about ritual purity and whether one follows the written word or the oral tradition. Jesus here gave three reasons why one should not allow the interpretations of the "elders" to govern behavior.

First, the quotation from Isaiah 29:13 (in Mark 7:6-8) sets up a distinction between being outwardly pious and honoring God in one's heart. Jesus' opponents did what Isaiah criticized: They set aside a teaching they should keep ("Honor your father and mother") and kept one they should set aside. They abandoned God's commandment in favor of their (pious) tradition.

Second, *corban* was a custom in which one vowed one's property to God. It may have been much like what we do when we make a large endowment to an institution but have the right to live on the money during our lifetimes. Could one actually be released from this vow to meet the needs of aged parents? Both the rabbis and Jesus said yes—the commandment took precedence over the vow.

When Jesus "drilled down" here, he criticized the hypocrisy of those who took shelter behind pious words to avoid caring for elderly parents. Mark 7:13 generalizes from this argument to include all interpretation opposed to the Word of God. (Of course, for us there is still the question of interpreting which words within the Word take precedence!)

Third, Jesus called the crowd back together

and began to teach with authority. In verse 15, he tackled the question of ritual purity head-on. Impurity is not something that has to do with legal rules and practices; it is something that comes from within. Recall that Jesus was not concerned about being made ritually impure because of his contact with the leper or with the woman with the continuous bleeding. He was concerned about their needs first and foremost. Mark's "aside" in verse 19 made clear the practical consequences of this argument for his readers.

Look more closely at Mark 7:17-23. This comment not only radicalized the dietary laws, it struck at the heart of religious hypocrisy. With a partner or privately in your journal, reflect on these practices that feed "evil intentions." What practices do you need to change? Have you rationalized (or hidden behind the letter of the law) to keep from having to change?

The Seven Last Words of the Church

The reality is, for all human beings in all times and places, it is much easier to follow the rituals and traditions than it is to commit our hearts to faithful discipleship. There is the old joke about "the seven last words of the church"; that is, "We've never done it that way before." We tend to hang on to traditions as if they were divinely revealed.

However, in the last 150 years in the United States, we have "drilled-down" past the biblical statements approving slavery to the radical truth that God does not will one human being to own another. We have "drilled-down" past Paul's statements about women keeping silent in the church to the radical truth that God calls both men and women to ministry of all kinds in the church. What issues in our day call for us to "drill-down" past traditions and even texts of Scripture to what God calls us to become in the twenty-first century?

The Seven Last Words . . .

Quickly call out and list your favorite traditions or the events, attitudes, and behaviors that your church (or you) cherishes. About what has your church said, "We've never done it that way" in order to keep from even trying something new?

What is being preserved in these instances? What made that important in the first place? Is the reason still relevant?

How might Jesus challenge that tradition today? Is there any reason to move into a new method or ideal? Why and for what purpose?

"You Search the Scriptures . . ."

One point of difference between the early Christian church and the Jewish synagogue was over the interpretation of Scripture, as John 5:39 shows. The community for whom

"You Search the Scriptures . . ."

At the heart of some theological debate today is the question of whether Scripture is the closed

John was written struggled with the synagogue just as Matthew's community did and finally felt they had to leave, because the way they understood Jesus made it impossible for them to stay. Their feelings are summed up in this saying: The Scriptures are not the final word but point beyond themselves to Jesus.

The heart of the question was that the early Christian church believed God's revelation in Jesus built on and went beyond the witness in written Scripture. They were clear that God's revelation continued beyond the Scripture. Today, one of the great divides in the Christian church is over that question, which seemed so clear to our ancestors. Did God say everything that God ever intended to say about every issue in the written words of Scripture? Or does God continue to reveal new insights and wisdom to the church? This question is at the heart of many of the divisions in the church today—and there seems to be no easy way to come to an understanding about it.

This leads us to the ultimate real-life question for this chapter: What do we believe about the interpretation and the authority of Scripture? When we say it is the Word of God, what do we mean? We have seen, from Jesus' example, that taking the Scripture literally, instead of seeking for its ultimate meaning, can put us in a box of legalistic interpretation. Hanging on to traditional ideas can cause us to miss what the Scripture really wants to say to us. So how do we interpret Scripture?

Word of God or if God continues to speak and reveal new insights.

What do you think about whether God's revelation is on-going? What theological justification do you have for your stance? If God speaks to us today, how do we hold that in tension with the Scripture? What does your answer say about what you believe about God? What do you believe about the authority of Scripture? Why do you believe that?

Close With Prayer

It may be that this discussion has stirred up strong feelings and perhaps left some anger, resentment, or concern among group members.

Summarize the main points, including any points of contention. Offer these issues in prayer, including a prayer for the discernment of God's will. Close with petitions for openness, respect, and love for all persons.

Session Five

Making Trouble on Three Levels

1-2-3

In our struggles to be Christian in the world, we live and function on at least three levels. For example, we hear Jesus' command to feed the hungry (Matthew 25:31-36). How do we respond to that command? On one level, we do our part to feed the hungry. We write a check. We bring canned goods to the church for the local food bank. We contribute to the "100 Neediest Cases" or drop an extra dollar into the Salvation Army kettle at Christmas time. Those are legitimate ways to respond to the command to feed the hungry.

What About the Poor and Hungry?

We make a mistake if we assume that everyone in the church is (1) in a position to help those who are poor and hungry and (2) are not poor or hungry themselves. The mainline churches in the US are often affluent; indeed the facilities and staff of many congregations require a moneyed constituency. But that does not mean that individual members are never themselves in need, even those who are employed and who own a home. Does the gospel command those who "have not" or "have little" to give to others in need?

Session Focus

The session focuses on moving beyond doing good to working for justice.

Session Objective

To see Jesus as a change agent and to learn the importance of systemic changes as a key to justice.

Session Preparation

Gather newspapers (enough so each member of the group will have a complete section) and masking tape. Have on hand a Bible dictionary and some hymnals.

Choose from among these activities and discussion starters to plan your lesson.

1-2-3

Choose a life issue that is important to most of the group members. Identify three or four things that you do on level one to care for that issue.

The Poor and Hungry

In "round robin" fashion, take an inventory of

assumptions that you have of the church and its members. Is the picture of the church that emerges a homogeneous one or is there great variety? Then think about your facility and minimal budget requirements (just, for example, to have building and a pastor). Can your church be a church of the poor?

Level Two

At a deeper level, we get involved in feeding the hungry. We recognize that they are a part of God's people, our brothers and sisters. Perhaps, at a visceral level that we do not admit even to ourselves, we recognize what a fine line separates the needy from those who have sufficient resources. (How many persons do we know who are one or two paychecks or disasters from the street?)

When we feed a brother or sister or someone we know, writing a check or giving some canned goods no longer seems enough. We become involved with the hungry as people. We work in the soup kitchen or the homeless shelter. We come to know that these are not just "the hungry"; these are people with names and stories and hopes. Some of the barriers come down, and we begin to operate out of love and understanding.

Level Two

Return to the life issue identified earlier and brainstorm "level two" activities that you have actually done. How have they changed the way you understood that issue?

Level Three

At a still deeper level, we begin to ask: Why is it, in the richest nation in the history of the world, that anyone has to be hungry? What's wrong with the economic/social/political system that some people are left out of the economic good times?

So we begin to study, to become involved with public interest groups, to write letters to congresspersons and government agencies. We try to enlist our friends, our Sunday school class, our service club, in the effort to deal with root causes of hunger. It is at this level that we begin to be troublemakers.

"Doing good" is not always enough. The good Samaritan has always been lifted up as a model for how to care for our neighbor in need. He is a model for that neighbor. But what if, every time he made the trip from Jerusalem to Jericho, there had been another

Level Three

Distribute the newspaper sections. Review all three levels at which we live and function in the world.

Tear out articles and tape them onto poster board or post them as a montage. Look for stories that illustrate dealing with human need on one or more of the three levels. Identify the three levels in the articles.

Do you ever wonder about the "fine line" that separates our situation from that of persons who are hungry, homeless, or otherwise in need? How close are we to being on the other side of that line? What happens to us when

battered victim lying in the ditch? Perhaps we would see the Samaritan at Roman headquarters, lobbying for more police protection on that road and maybe even ambulance service with EMTs. We also love our neighbor when we work to change the system that hurts or oppresses the neighbor.

we see "the hungry" as our brothers and sisters? What happens in our relationship with them? Why is "doing good" sometimes not enough?

Changing the System

There were all kinds of people in Jesus' day who wanted to change the political/economic/social system. The Zealots (the revolutionary underground) wanted to change the system by starting a war and driving out the hated Roman oppressors.

Changing the System

Very briefly jot down a few definitions or similes for *radical.* "A radical is ____ or a radical is like ____." *Do not discuss them yet.*

The Zealots

The Zealots were first of all motivated by a radical zeal for the one true God and for God's law. Taking as their banner God's self-description in the Ten Commandments, "I the LORD your God am a jealous God" (Exodus 20:5), the Zealots were willing not only to die for the sake of the law, but also to take the life of another Israelite who failed to uphold it.

The mission of the Zealots was in some sense cleansing and restorative, as when a surgeon excises cancerous tissue to save the body. Zealots saw themselves as God's agents against apostasy, idolatry, and any other transgression of the law. As strict guardians of the institution of their forefathers and foremothers, there was no foe of the true faith too fearsome or trivial to ignore.

Bible 301: Zealots

Using a Bible dictionary, look up Zealot. Zealot *and* jealous *have the same linguistic root. If God is a jealous God, are we also called to be zealous for God's will and law? Why or why not? What, if any, are the boundaries for that zeal? Have you ever thought about religious zeal as being cleansing and restorative, as in excising a cancer? Is this a good thing or dangerous or neither? Why?*

The Pharisees wanted to change the system by righteous living. They believed that, if all Israel would just keep Torah perfectly

Review all the information about the Pharisees. If the Pharisees comprised just a small percentage of the population, why would their religious observance be expected to have such influence on Jewish life?

for one day, then Messiah would come, and the world would be different. (No wonder the Pharisees were always so upset with people, including Jesus, who didn't take their interpretation of Torah seriously enough.)

The Pharisees

How does the notion of Pharisaic observance as just one aspect of religious life change your perspective on its importance? on the expectation that Jesus' religious and faith expression should conform to their ritual practices?

The Pharisees

There is no uniform scholarly agreement on the origin of the Pharisees, who made up a small percentage of the Jewish population. The seeds of Pharisaism were sown during the Exile, several centuries before the birth of Jesus, when the Temple was destroyed. Deprived of the locus of worship, the Law (Torah) became central to the Jewish religion and supplied the pattern for Jewish life. The Law was the soul of the nation.

When the exiles returned and rebuilt the Temple, the stage was set for the observance of Torah that could stand alone, even in opposition to the Temple, if need be. There arose "doctors of the Law," nonpriestly interpreters and preservers who owed no allegiance to the Temple.

Four centuries later, when the influence of Greek culture was being thrust brutally upon the Jews, the Law was a rallying point for Jewish loyalty. The religious backbone of resistance came from the Hasidim, the pious assembly comprised (probably) of priestly scribes and lay lawyers. Their adamant refusal to capitulate to Hellenism was at the heart of the Jewish resistance. Those who remained with the Temple and capitulated to their Greek conquerors were the forebears of the Sadducees; the separatists became the forebears of the Pharisees.

The Pharisees and Zealots had a great stake in the law and the institutions that upheld it. What service did they perform for their faith and its adherents?

Clearly, there were forces within the religious and social culture who, from the fiber of their being, were intent on upholding the Torah. The Pharisees and Zealots were culturally and historically steeped in the preservation of the commandments and the way of life determined by adherence to God's law. It is no wonder that they resisted anyone or anything they perceived as a threat to God's chosen people and the sustaining system.

Even those who were on the margins of the system, the *anawim*, just wanted a little relief from the day-to-day misery of their lives. These poor of the land, whom we met in Session One, would have been happy for any change in the system that gave them a little job security, a little relief from taxes, a little better diet, a little hope that things might be better for their children.

Then there was Jesus himself. He also wanted to change the system. He called his proposal for changing the system the kingdom of God. He said that, when men and women entered into the Kingdom, they became new people and began to live in different ways—meaning that the society around them would change too.

How did Zealots and Pharisees want to change the system? Is there any more or less desire for change when changing back (as in the Zealots' desire for upholding the letter of the Law as given in its earliest days) or when changing in the particulars (as the Pharisees' penchant for codifying more and more minute ramifications or applications of a single law) or when calling for a reinterpretation of the law (as Jesus did)? Explain.

What are some modern parallels to the Zealots and Pharisees? How are they regarded by the "mainstream"? Discuss the images of "radical" that you listed earlier. To whom and with what effect could you apply the term in the church today?

Why Change the System?

Of course, there were also some people who didn't want to change anything about the system. The Romans were perfectly happy with the way things were. The oppressor, the incumbent, the one with the reins of power, is generally intent on maintaining the status quo. Change would involve the increase of power. The Sadducees and the other Jewish nobles saw no reason to change anything. They had the power (economic and religious), the wealth, the social position, and saw no reason to give up any of it.

For those on the under side of the system, there were reasons for change. The commandments and laws of Israel clearly indicate a responsibility to be faithful to God and to

Why Change the System?

How would you describe the "system"? Are you only in one system or many? If more than one, what are they? Is your position different in one system than another? If so, what is the difference in terms of your influence on and influence by the system? Are you, personally, comfortable with the system? Why or why not? Why would it be hard for us to work to change something that makes us comfortable?

care for the "least." When their political, social, or economic system caused pain or suffering for people, the system no longer worked the way it should have, and it needed to be changed. We saw, in Session One, clear evidence of the way the system was not working in Jesus' day.

Read Deuteronomy 24:6-22 for a sample of the laws that protect the weak and vulnerable. How does law/government in the US provide for the vulnerable? Is this care something to which persons are entitled (which means protection would be "embedded" in our laws and constitution)?

Deeply embedded in the thought of the people of Israel was the conviction that the primary function of government was to protect and take care of those persons who could not take care of themselves. All through the Torah, there are references to caring for widows and orphans (see, for example, Deuteronomy 24:17-22). These were people (more like "nonpeople," in the culture of that day) who had no legal, political, social, or economic standing. They lived on the margins of society, trying to scrape together enough grain to get through one more day.

Review the Scriptures from the Psalms and Amos about the responsibility of the king and other national leaders. What mandate do they have in terms of caring for the general population? What is the function of the king? What is God's word to those who do not fulfill their responsibilities? What would our government look like if it were modeled on Scripture? Is this reasonable or feasible? If not, what responsibility and options do we have for caring for the vulnerable in our society?

The psalmists sang the praises of kings at their coronations, reminding them that they were called to act for God on behalf of the oppressed in society. (See Psalms 58; 72:1-4; 82; 101, for example.) The great prophets called for all the people of Israel to be just in their dealings with the poor. Amos, for example, denounced the practice of selling children into slavery to pay debts, or driving farmers off the land because of their poverty (Amos 2:6-7). That's the meaning behind his denunciation of those who "sell . . . the needy for a pair of sandals" (Amos 2:6). What kind of just system puts the value of a human life on a par with the value of a pair of shoes?

And what about us? Ask: what systems in our society abuse or oppress people? In what way? What do you think God would want in

The prophets called for all God's people to live with justice and mercy for the poor and oppressed. Indeed, the concept of justice in the prophets seems grounded in a love for

those situations? What stake do we have in "the way things are"?

neighbor that does not take advantage of the system to oppress the neighbor. When justice and mercy failed, then the prophets condemned the wealthy for the way they got and abused their wealth and promised God's judgment on those who did not take their responsibility for the poor neighbor seriously. (See, for example, Isaiah 10:1-4.)

That's why we work to change the system—the system is either imperfect, or it is abused, or both. When that happens, God's concern for the poor calls us to change the system to make it more equitable.

Jesus Challenged the System

Note the three levels:
- Direct help, such as healing
- Opening up the community
- Offering a new way to think about or interact with the system

Read Mark 1:40-45 and 5:25-34 as an overview of how these levels can work. What level one activity are you or your church doing regularly?

Jesus Challenged the System on Three Levels

As the Son of God, Jesus challenged the system in a kind of "drill-down" in action. First, he helped people who were in distress, just like the good Samaritan did. Take two examples: the leper (Mark 1:40-45) and the woman with the hemorrhage (Mark 5:25-34). At the most obvious level, he dealt with their physical needs—he healed their sickness. That's what churches, service clubs, and other do when they send doctors to areas where there is inadequate medical care, when they arrange for persons to come to hospitals in the United States (or in a teaching hospital in the city) for operations they could never have at home, even if they could afford them.

A Leprous Man

Turn again to Mark 1:40-45 and to Leviticus 13-14. In small groups, skim through the two chapters in Leviticus to get a better understanding of the diseases covered, their purification rites, and the role of the priests in cleansing.

Level Two: Healing a Leprous Man

Jesus "drilled-down" to a second level. He not only healed people, he opened up the community to them. The lepers were cast out of the community because they were (or were considered to be) contagious and unclean. They could not worship, buy or sell, or even visit with their friends or families. Persons who came into contact with them also became unclean and had to wait out a period of purification (quarantine) to be sure they did not also have the disease (Leviticus 13–14). The fact that Jesus touched a leper was enough to make him ritually unclean.

Have you ever had to be quarantined, stranded somewhere remote, or set apart from your family or other community? What did that time of isolation feel like? What did you think about it?

Bible 301: Leprosy ☐

Look up leprosy *in a Bible dictionary for a more comprehensive understanding of how skin disease, including leprosy, was regarded and treated.*

"Leprosy"

Leviticus devoted two entire chapters to scale disease, complete with detailed instructions for how to care for various skin disorders and their symptoms. No doubt, many skin diseases, such as vitiligo or perhaps psoriasis, that were characterized by scaling, peeling, change of color, or discharge, were labeled as leprosy. The regulations of Leviticus make the distinction between curable and incurable diseases. Those who exhibited the typical symptoms for leprosy were required to "wear torn clothes, and let the hair of [their] head be disheveled." As long as one had the disease, "he shall cover his upper lip and cry out, 'Unclean, unclean.' He shall remain unclean as long as he has the disease; he is unclean. He shall live alone; his dwelling shall be outside the camp" (Leviticus 13:45-46).

"Lepers" were expelled from the camp for religious rather than medical reasons. Leviticus offers an elaborate series of sacrifices and rituals for cleansing before a diseased person could be healed and returned to the community.

How did Jesus treat the leper? What were the implications for Jesus touching him or even being in his presence, since he was not a priest? How did he challenge the law and sensibilities of his community in this healing? What are our own understandings of what is "clean" and "unclean" (either medically or culturally)? Who are the untouchables in our society? How do we treat them? What provision do we make for restoration to the community for them, if any? If we choose to leave them isolated, how can we justify it?

Priests were allowed to examine lepers (and anything else, such as garments or walls) that were considered leprous. Because the leper had to isolate himself, the Law provided that no one else would be able (or willing) to touch him. Jesus ignored this provision for maintaining ritual purity when he healed the man (Mark 1:41). Jesus restored him to the community. Restoration is behind the command to the leper to show himself to the priest and get the certificate of cleanliness (1:42-44).

Level Two: Healing the Hemorraghic Woman

The Hemorraghic Woman

Review Mark 5:25-34 and read Leviticus 12:2, 5; 15:19-30.

What happened in this healing? How was the woman healed? What plan and assumptions were in her mind leading up to the healing? In what ways was her disease disabling? isolating? Aside from the obvious benefit of feeling better, what did the woman stand to gain from taking the risk of making Jesus unclean?

The woman with the continuous flow of blood was also considered unclean (Mark 5:25-26). According to Torah, blood was sacred, but menstrual blood was a powerful taboo (Leviticus 12:2, 5; 15:19-30). Women had to be separate from the community during the days each month they were menstruating or having any other discharge. (This is also true of many other cultures.) Since this woman never stopped bleeding, she had been ostracized from the community for over eighteen years!

Even to touch Jesus' clothes as she did was enough to make Jesus ritually unclean. No one was permitted to touch her, her garments, her bedclothes, or the furniture upon which she sat. Contact with contaminated items made the person who had touched the item unclean until sundown. More than that, "If any man lies with her . . . he shall be unclean seven days" (15:24), which would also include a sabbath. Males would have a great incentive to keep their distance. Her disease was very isolating.

What are the implications of Jesus calling the woman, "Daughter"? In pairs or privately, consider a time when you were (or felt) cut off from something (or everything) precious and important to you. Imagine your feelings of isolation, perhaps fear or desperation. Now imagine Jesus coming to you, in defiance of the situation

Jesus healed the woman (inadvertently), but he also did more. He called her "daughter," and welcomed her back into the community (Mark 5:34). This is a major point at which Jesus challenged the system. It's almost as if he said, "Unclean? These are

and perhaps of important people, to lift you out of that isolation.

What would it mean for you to consider yourself a daughter (or son)?

God's children who are suffering. Shouldn't we do everything we can for them?" So he said to the lepers, "Go to the priests, show them you're clean, and get from them the certificate that will allow you to become a part of the community again" (see Mark 1:44). To the woman, he said, "Daughter."

Level Three: Acceptance

How did what Jesus did, or didn't do, demonstrate the acceptance of the person whom he healed and to whom he ministered?

Level Three: Acceptance in the System

The third level of this action "drill-down" was to demonstrate a new way to think about the system. Jesus didn't picket the Temple to get these people accepted again. He did not ask them to pay or to beg him or to debase themselves; they were not called to repent or to change. He just declared them accepted. He welcomed the outcast back into the community, which in itself was a challenge to the system.

Bible 301

Read through Mark 2:1–3:6 to see how Mark has summarized several controversial activities of Jesus and the response of the authorities to him. What does the unified effort of the Pharisees and Herodians represent?

Mark has helpfully told his reader in advance the reaction to this healing and Jesus' challenge to the system. In a series of short, powerful vignettes, Mark mentions five controversies (including healing the man with leprosy) that stood Jesus in poor stead with the sticklers for the law.

- Claiming authority to forgive sins (Mark 2:1-12)
- Calling a tax collector (2:13-17)
- Disputing with the Pharisees about fasting (2:18-22)
- Reinterpreting the sabbath (2:23-28)
- Healing on the sabbath (3.1-5)

Review how the "drill down in action" worked for Jesus. How did Jesus challenge the system on all three levels? Given the threat (Mark 3:6), what does his challenge suggest as an example for us?

From that point, Mark tells us, "the Pharisees went out and immediately conspired with the Herodians against him, how to destroy him" (3:6). An added danger is implied by yoking these unholy partners. In virtually any other endeavor, the Pharisees and Herodians would have been vigorous foes. To Mark, and surely to his readers, this pair would symbolize a comprehensive attack from both religious and civil authorities. Every other challenge that Mark reports is done against the backdrop of this threat. The Pharisees and Herodians would change or disregard the person. Jesus would shake up the system and models for us the courage to confront whatever disrespects, discards, or devalues what God considers valuable.

The Good Shepherd

Read Luke 15:1-6. Then sing or read together any of the hymns or songs about the Good Shepherd. (Look in your hymnal index for songs based on Psalm 23, for example.) How does the image of Jesus as shepherd comfort you? relate to your own life? confuse you? help or hinder your understanding of him?

Review the parable. Who was Jesus' audience? How does Mark characterize them or place them on his "stage of action"? How would that positioning have affected his audience's understanding of the importance of what Jesus did?

Who are the lost? Is it possible that the lost were lost *to* the religious environ-

The Good Shepherd

One of the best-loved of Jesus' parables is the good shepherd, who leaves the ninety-nine sheep and goes out to find the one who is lost (Luke 15:1-6). We get all sentimental over pictures of the shepherd, we sings songs about "The Ninety and Nine." We think this is such a wonderful thing that we miss how this parable challenges the system.

First, verses 1-2 describe Jesus' audience. Luke mentioned the tax collectors and sinners before he listed anyone else. The next on the guest list are the Pharisees and the scribes. Luke set them apart by indicating that the "dregs" of society were there, eagerly listening, and the "righteous" were there, grumbling.

Jesus' parable is a direct response to this grumbling by those of the "inner circle" about the castoffs. The clear implication is that those who considered themselves the best were the ones left in the wilderness (to fend for themselves?) while the shepherd went off in search of the "one that is lost." Is it possible that *lost* means "lost to the religious establishment," or even, "lost *by* the religious establishment"?

Anyone who is excluded from the community, anyone who is cast out, who is left on the margins, is that one lost sheep for whom

ment (such as those isolated by leprosy or continuous bleeding) or lost *by* the religious environment (such as those whom the Pharisees or Zealots would condemn, correct, or even kill)?

How is the parable of the Good Shepherd a challenge to the system? How does it challenge the church? How does it challenge you?

Really "Rotten" People

What does the old saying about rotten apples and the barrel say? What does that mean for you?

In four small groups, review the Scriptures that refer to Matthew, Zacchaeus, the accused woman, and the accused Jesus. How did Jesus' behavior or associations "make trouble"? Would you call that trouble, really? For whom was it trouble? Imagine (or act out) that you are on the board of a civic group, or the homeowners association, or the church, or the school. Someone has been accused, beyond doubt, of breaching the group's ethics and policies. Jesus has brought that person before the board and is asking the members (and you) to restore that person to a good standing, just

the shepherd seeks. That is, Jesus suggests he leaves all of us good people in the fold and goes out after the homeless woman and her children; the drug addict sleeping under the bridge, the teenager with purple hair who is trying to find love, the gay couple who have just been turned away by the church, the illegal immigrant, and all the others whom we would like to ignore.

That is a challenge to the system! Particularly when we get the feeling Jesus goes after these lost sheep and then looks at us and says, "go and do likewise."

Really "Rotten" People

Jesus made trouble by hanging out with really "rotten" people. Just look at some of the people he called to follow him. There was Matthew, the tax collector (Matthew 9:9-13); Zacchaeus, another tax collector who cheated people so much that he had to make restitution at 400 percent (Luke 19:1-10); the woman taken in adultery (John 8:2-11). Jesus was accused of being a glutton and a drunkard because he hung out with the wrong crowd (Matthew 11:16-19; Luke 7: 31-35). The word from the religious in-crowd was that Jesus was out because he talked to prostitutes and other sinners.

But, with these people, Jesus followed the same three steps. First, he dealt with their immediate problem. He saved the woman taken in adultery from death by stoning. He took Matthew away from the tax collector's table. He called Zacchaeus down from the tree. Then he drilled-down to the second level and made them part of the community again.

To the woman taken in adultery, he said, "Where are [your accusers]? . . . Neither do I condemn you. Go your way, and from now

because he is asking. (If you wish, use one of the Bible stories as the model or as the actual case to consider.)

What process would you use to deliberate on his request? What information would you ask for? What factors might weigh more heavily than others in the decision-making? If you regarded Jesus as just another hometown man, instead of the Son of God, how would you weight his influence and desire in your process?

Restoration

Think again about the systems of which you are a part and who is shunted outside the system.

What factors place them or you outside the system? What change in behavior, values, attitudes, or processes would result in restoration of their place in the system? in the restoration or re-creation of a better system? What value is there in being a part of the system? of being apart from it?

on, do not sin again" (John 8:10-11). With the charges against her lifted, she could resume her rightful place in the community. Jesus went from the marketplace where Matthew was collecting taxes to a party at Matthew's home, saying by his very presence that Matthew was part of the people of God (Matthew 9:10). He went to Zacchaeus's house for dinner and then, in the presence of the crowd, said that Zacchaeus, too, was a son of Abraham (Luke 19:9). He said to the Pharisees that prostitutes and tax collectors would go into the Kingdom ahead of them (Matthew 21:31-32). That's a radical new view of who's in and who's out!

Restoration: Change or Stay the Same

In every one of those actions, Jesus scandalized the community, because he challenged the very system that made these people outcasts in the first place. In some instances, persons were asked or offered to change. Jesus did not come preaching "Repent" for nothing. When sinful behavior was a barrier to the right life with God, Jesus empowered and encouraged persons to change.

In other instances, disease or disenfranchisement imposed from outside formed the barrier. To these persons, such as the woman with the hemorrhage and the leper, Jesus held out the hand of healing, welcome, and restoration. In all these cases, Jesus placed the person before the institution. The goal was to restore the person to the community and to restore the community to a right relationship with God. Jesus challenged his own society and continues to challenge us to do the same.

So What About Us?

Those of us who have good jobs, good homes, stock and mutual fund portfolios, medical plans, retirement plans have a vested interest in the way the system works. We (many of us) belong to that group of persons who make decisions in the church, in business, schools, civic clubs, political life. We are the system. Why would we want to change that? Why would we want to challenge the system that takes such good care of us?

Others of us are what those in power positions might consider the underbelly. We need help from the system; we are perceived as taking more out that we put in. We drain the system. Some others "work" the system; others are leeches, the stereotypically lazy welfare "cheats." Jesus comes to us all. Even from the underside, there can be a certain familiar comfort in the status quo. Better the devil you know than the devil you don't, as the saying goes.

When Jesus challenged the rich young man to sell everything he had, give the money to the poor, and then come follow him, the young man went away in sorrow. Why? Because he couldn't challenge the system by walking away from it (Matthew 19:16-26; Mark 10:17-31; Luke 18:18-30). He had too much at stake in the way things were. Many of us do.

It is not sinful to recognize what stake we have in the status quo, whether we receive from it or are buffeted by it. Neither is it sinful to acknowledge how hard it is to work on changing a system that stands between us and God. But we do have to be honest—it's harder for us to follow Jesus when he makes that challenge.

So What About Us?

Read the story about the rich man in one of the Gospels. Put yourself in his place. List all the "stuff" you have that Jesus might ask you to give up in order to have an effective and uncluttered ministry. What stake do you have in keeping your life just as it is?

Next list all the possibilities that might arise if you took the leap and made the sacrifices. How enticing are these possibilities? How "radical" are they for you?

Next examine your heart. Is Jesus Christ leading you to this sort of change or commitment? Is there a part of the system that you need to work to change? someone who is left out or pushed out whom you would work to restore? someone who is working for restoration on your behalf whom you have failed to appreciate? Can you take up whatever challenge Jesus is presenting?

Close With Prayer

Summarize your insights about who is in and who is out of the systems and what stake we have in those systems. Offer prayers for the "lost" and for guidance about how God might be calling you. Close with prayer for discernment about systems and how God would want us to work to change them.

Session Six

Money

Just Talk

Jesus got in trouble because he talked about money. He told about a laborer's wages, a miser's bank account, a widow's mite, a pearl of great value. He made pronouncements about money and told jokes about the wealthy. Jesus blessed the poor and condemned the rich.

What does Jesus say that put him in so much trouble? Let's look at Scripture.

Greed

Read Luke 12:13-21.

Jesus says that we should not be greedy. "Take care! Be on your guard against all kinds of greed; for one's life does not consist in the abundance of possessions" (Luke 12:15). He told the story of a landowner who stored all his crops and his goods in bigger and bigger barns, saving for retirement. But God said to him, "This very night your life is being demanded of you. And the things you have prepared, whose will they be?" (Luke 12:20).

The question may be simple, but it reveals multiple failures or flaws in the man's thinking and behavior. Deuteronomic law required that he leave something for the gleaners; he wanted to keep "all [his] grain and [his] goods" (12:18). There was no problem with the abundance of his harvest; rather on his self-centered insistence on "my crops,

Session Focus ■
Jesus troubles us because he tells us to give away our possessions.

Session Objective ■
To be confronted by Jesus' demands about money and to begin making decisions about following Jesus.

Session Preparation ■
Be aware of your feelings as you listen to Jesus' demands about money and possessions. You will need a Bible commentary for some activities.

Choose from among these activities and discussion starters to plan your lesson.

Just Talk ■
What do you remember Jesus saying about money?

Greed ■
Read Luke 12:13-21. In what ways are you like the landowner? How do you save your money? What are you saving for? How do you feel when Jesus says, "This very night your life is being demanded of you"?

Invite volunteers to act out the story of this rich landowner, recasting it, if you wish, in an updated version. Given the reading and the re-enacting, how would you see the man's character. Is he just a hedonistic, practical atheist? Is he wrong for wanting to secure his future? Is the price he paid for his "me" attitude too steep? Explain your answers.

Consider the possibilities if "they" means God or the man's possessions. How could his possessions take his life? How might possessions take your life?

my barns, my grain, my goods, my future, my soul." It apparently did not occur to him that he had any responsibility for the poor.

In the midst of the man's hedonistic attitude about his own wealth and his own self-sufficiency, he demonstrated a kind of practical atheism. He may have given lip service to his belief in God and his appreciation for God's blessing, but he lived as if all were in his own power and control. The punch line of the parable stands in sharp contrast to the man's smug attitude. "This night" he lost not only his goods, but his life and soul as well.

Luke's choice of words leaves us with an interpretive puzzle and an interesting possibility. Luke wrote that "your life is being demanded of you"; the verb form ("they will demand") is generally taken to mean that "they" (God) will take the man's life. An alternative possibility is that "they" (the possessions) will take his life. In either case, the point is made. The man was possessed by his possessions and as a result, all was lost.

Our first response may be to laugh at the landowner's foolishness. Yet, this is a hard truth, for how many of us are just like he is? While some of us scrape to get by and others of us with discretionary income spend it charitably, many of us spend and accumulate generously for ourselves—toys, clothes, cars, homes and furnishings, vacations abroad, investments. Could it be that Jesus may someday say to us, at the height of our greedy consumption, "You fool! This very night your life is demanded of you"?

Don't Worry

Read Matthew 6:25-33. Summarize it in your own words.

Don't Worry

Read Matthew 6:25-33.

Jesus says, "Do not worry about your life, what you will eat or what you will drink, or about your body, what you will wear. Is not life more than food, and the body more than clothing? . . . Strive first for the kingdom of God and his righteousness, and all these things will be given to you as well" (Matthew 6:25, 33).

What does it mean to "strive first for the kingdom of God and his righteousness"? Does this mean that those who earnestly desire God and do God's will need not bother with an income or other "worldly" cares? Why or why not?

Since all of us "sow, reap," and so on, how can we avoid worry?

Is this passage about anxiety or priorities or something else?

Jesus' words are to the wealthy and to the poor. Those who have much can elevate their goods to a god-like status, but it is just as easy to idolize what we don't have and can't get. Yet in some way, all of us "sow, reap, store, toil, spin." Somehow, we have to take care of necessities: water, food, shelter, clothing. We work for a living to provide for ourselves and our families, to keep food on the table and a roof over our heads. Jesus never challenged this reality. Nevertheless, he says, "Don't worry about it."

Some interpreters say that the Scripture means that our spiritual lives are more important than our physical needs. We should set priorities. We shouldn't get so bogged down in making money that we forget to say our prayers. Other preachers say that Jesus is concerned about stress. "Don't worry," they say. "God will take care of you."

How would you describe the Kingdom message of this passage? If you understood the present age to be passing away quickly, would you interpret this passage any differently? If so, how?

Jesus says that we need to keep our priorities straight. He also says that God will provide. Jesus' message is first of all advice on practical piety. Take the day as it comes, with confidence that God wills that none of us should suffer want. But there is a Kingdom message beyond this. This loving God who holds our present also holds our future. God not only carries the whole world, including us; God will bring all to a worthy conclusion.

What responsibility do you feel you have to care for your neighbor? In what ways would loving neighbors change your financial situation? In what ways would it change you?

The rich man in the parable told by Luke lived his life selfishly, with no care for others; this unworthy lifestyle was cut short. Jesus comforts and guides us in this expression to place our priorities with God, where they belong, and to trust that God will make all things right. Until that time comes, we, as the rich landowner, have our responsibility to others as well as to ourselves.

Most of us need to spend forty hours a week at work, making money to support ourselves and our families. Jesus says to us that such is not our only task. Jesus expects us also to spend our time working for justice, building homes for the homeless, feeding the hungry, providing medical care for the indigent—instead of worrying about our own bellies and our own financial futures.

Either with one partner or privately as a journal exercise, do some figuring on how much money you spend on yourself and on your family. ("Guesstimate" that taxes take up the first four months or so of your income.) How would you feel if Jesus asked you to give away 25 percent of your income? 50 percent of your income? What do you think: Does Jesus ask us to be poor?

The Economy

Whenever Jesus talks about money, he speaks to corporations and nations as well as to individuals. He addresses the United States, where CEOs make salaries in six and seven figures and young adults have cars and CDs and designer clothing, where the economy is based on the whim of consumers and on competition for market niches. Greed defines many of us. When Jesus says, "Change your priorities. God will provide," he is not just talking to us, he is talking to a nation.

Bible 301: The Economy

As you read the remainder of the Scripture passages, keep in mind that they are intended for the entire community, not just individually. Read up on Matthew 19:16–20:16 in a Bible commentary, such as The New Interpreter's Bible, *Volume VIII (Abingdon Press, 1995).*

Give it Away; Follow Me

Read Matthew 19:16-30, a story that we at first believe is just about an individual. A rich man came to Jesus and asked, "Teacher, what good deed must I do to have eternal life?" Jesus answered, "If you wish to enter into life, keep the commandments." Then Jesus added, "If you wish to be perfect ["whole," "mature," as in 5:48], go, sell your possessions, and give the money to the poor, . . . then come, follow me."

It isn't the first time Jesus called disciples to give up their possessions. Think of Peter, Andrew, James, and John, who left not only

Give It Away; Follow Me

Read Matthew 19:16-30 and the parallel accounts in Mark 10:17-22 and Luke 18:18-24. (You will come back to the camel later!)

Note how the rich man phrased his question in the Gospel of Matthew: "What good deed must I do?" and the added response in Mark, "You shall not defraud." What do these specifics add to your understanding of the story?

How would you describe the rich man today? (The Gospel writers resist the temptation to portray him as evil.)

How do you feel when Jesus says, "Go, sell what you have, and give the money to the poor, . . .then come, follow me"? How would you respond? What does discipleship require?

Imagine what would happen if all wealthy people sold all their possessions and gave the money to the poor. How would the world change?

Does this Scripture scare you? If you take it seriously as a call to put off any claim to self-sufficiency, will you go away sorrowful as the rich man or rejoicing at the sacrifice? Why?

their possessions but their livelihood to follow Jesus (see Mark 1:16-20). When Jesus called Levi, he got up, left his tax booth, and followed (Mark 2:13-14). Called to follow Jesus, the disciples gave up all they had. Discipleship means surrendering oneself, including one's possessions, to God and God's will.

Jesus speaks to all the wealthy—people, corporations, and nations. Imagine how the world would change if the rich sold all they had and gave to the poor! Nations wouldn't quibble over raising taxes for the rich or expanding services for the poor. Billionaires would distribute their wealth. Social climbing would give way to philanthropy. Jesus' demands come from a vision of a world economy based on loving neighbors. So he commands us to give away everything. "Sell what you have; give to the poor."

The Scripture scares us, so we try to soften Jesus' words. Or we take comfort in thinking that they were only for the wealthy or for persons whose greed interfered with their discipleship. But if we realize that they are intended for the community—the man and the poor who continued to suffer because of his selfishness—then this message has to include all others as well. Jesus spoke to all who would reject God's grace in favor of personal justification and self-sufficiency, as did the sincere young man who sought salvation through his deeds (19:16). That, Jesus said, is impossible; and all such "young men" go away confused and sorrowful.

The Last Will Be First

Read Matthew 20:1-16. Consider the surface implications of this parable that can address how we

The Last Will Be First

Read Matthew 20:1-15. Jesus talks about God's kingdom, which turns everything upside down. "The last will be first," says Jesus, "and the first will be last" (20:16).

approach economic practices and attitudes.

Consider this parable first only by its surface implications. The story is about temporary laborers, standing on the corner, hoping for work. Early in the day, the first group is hired, after bargaining for a day's wages. They have an actual contract for their work. The second group, hired later in the day, will be paid "fairly"; but *fairly* is not defined and they must rely on the good word of the employer. The last group is the people who, at the last hour of the workday, anticipate that they and their families will go hungry that night.

What are the issues of fairness and justice in this passage? What does it mean in practical terms that the last will be first and the first, last?

When the paychecks are written, they're all the same. The landowner pays each person a full day's wage. We can't help but question the landowner's economic values. Our question is what the first group of workers would ask: "What happened to equal pay for equal work?" "How is one hour of work 'fair' when that pays the same as twelve hours?"

Note that this comment was made twice (Matthew 19:30 and 20:16). What is the context for each saying? Can you see yourself in this statement? Why or why not?

The landowner's irritation is evident in his use of a distancing form of address, "Friend." "Can't I do as I please? Do you question my generosity?" he asks. "So," Jesus repeats, "the last will be first, and the first will be last" (20:16; see also 19:30).

Form several small groups and imagine that each group is a different-sized business or corporation. Identify which group is which size, state what its annual budget is, and begin to design an economic system based on loving neighbors. How would you structure a vision statement for your company? a budget? your staff? your company goals? How, do you think, would this affect your bottom line?

Taken at surface value, we are forced to acknowledge that our economic systems are not God's. God's kingdom is not based on work or ambition or climbing the corporate ladder or management systems. God is neither a socialist nor a capitalist. God's economic systems are based on loving neighbors. Imagine an economy based on generosity!

What would happen if our economy were based on loving neighbors? Perhaps corporations would worry less about the bottom line and more about giving to the poor. Maybe governments would forgive the debts of third-world nations struggling to survive.

Jesus tells us in the parable that things will change.

Taken to its deeper meaning, the parable reaffirms the message to the rich man who rejected God's grace in favor of self-justification. The good employer's behavior highlights the resentment of grace by those who also sought to justify themselves by their good deeds (20:12; see also 19:16-20).

The first-hired laborers did not at first object to the grace others had been shown, but to the fact that they then expected more than was bargained for and didn't get it. They received their due according to the employer's justice. The last-hired received their wage—they were made "equal"—by grace.

Now examine the parable from the viewpoint of the imminent Kingdom. The work of the harvest has to be done *now*, with as many workers as are available, or all is lost. When the Kingdom comes, what will the "reward" structure look like? What is the place for amassing treasure? for expecting to be made equal to others or having them made equal to us? for feelings of resentment at God's graciousness?

Whether we take the initial or the deeper meaning, the implication of Jesus' teaching to the young man and to the hearers of the parable is clear. Our attitude and behavior is to be motivated by grace and generosity, not by greed or self-service. In God's kingdom, expectations of self-advancement are turned upside down.

Jesus Says ■

Write a statement summarizing what Jesus says about money. Note that Luke 8:1-3 says that many people, including several women, traveled with Jesus and provided for him out of their means. Either they did not give up everything, or they gave all of it over to support Jesus' itinerant ministry. But Luke 14:33 seems to say something different. How would you reconcile these Scriptures? Could there be two different kinds of disciples? Can

Jesus Says

Jesus repeated that teaching in multiple ways. "You cannot serve God and wealth," he said (Luke 16:13). Faith and greed are mutually exclusive. Faith means trusting God to provide and serving God by loving neighbors. If we are faithful, we cannot put heart and soul into supporting ourselves or putting aside a little for our future. To serve God, to follow Jesus, means giving up all that we own. "None of you can become my disciple," says Jesus, "if you do not give up all your possessions" (Luke 14:33).

Jesus also says that economic systems will change. No longer will a handful of people

you be a faithful disciple *and* keep resources for your own use?

Now write another statement expressing your response to what Jesus says.

control the world's checkbooks while the poor live on pocket change. Wealth will be redistributed.

E. F. Schumacher, in *Small Is Beautiful* (HarperCollins, 1989), says, "Call a thing immoral or ugly, soul-destroying or a degradation of man, a peril to the peace of the world or to the well-being of future generations; as long as you have not shown it to be 'uneconomic' you have not really questioned its right to exist, grow, and prosper."

Jesus says, "Change." Change the way you feel about money. Change the ways you earn money and the ways you spend money. CHANGE—writ large.

Trouble ■

Take a look at the Census Bureau figures. The upper income limit of households in 1999 by quintile (fifths) is widely disparate. The lowest fifth was $17,196; the second quintile $32,000; the third quintile $50,520; the fourth quintile $79,375. In which fifth does your household fall? How much of the consumer credit debt is yours and what is the percentage of debt compared to total income? What would Jesus say to you about that ratio?

Consider the images of possessions from around the world. Make a list of as many of your possessions as you can in two minutes. How much of it could you give away or live without? What makes you keep it? What would you want in your picture for this magazine? What would that say

Trouble

The problem, of course, is that we like our money. We're rather like the mad scientist, his shadow falling over a map of the world, as he shouts, "Mine! Mine! Mine!"

According to the Census Bureau, in 1999, the middle quintile (20 percent) of households had an annual income between $32,000 and $50,520. (The bottom 20 percent had a maximum annual income just over $17,000 and the top 5 percent had a minimum of $142,000.) The total outstanding consumer credit was nearly $1.4 trillion. By contrast, in Asia, the number of people living on $365 a year or less was expected to double by the year 2000.

Several years ago, a book (*Material World: A Global Family Portrait*, by Peter Menzel; Sierra Club Books, 1994) printed a series of pictures showing what people in different nations owned. A woman huddled under a red scarf; she sat on a pallet woven of straw and nursed her child. A man dressed in robes, like Abraham, and carrying a staff, stood on a hand-tied rug. Ten pots were lined up on the edge of the rug. A man in

about you and your priorities? What would Jesus say about that?

shorts and a golf shirt sat on the hood of his car. The car was parked with another in a driveway, in front of a brick home. A basketball hoop hung above the garage door. Other belongings—clothes, shoes, appliances, golf clubs, bicycles, boxes of books, a computer, two televisions, a CD player and a collection of CDs, china, pots and pans, rugs, sofas, tables—filled the garage, the driveway, the yard. Americans have a lot of possessions! There's no doubt about it; most Americans love the money we have and would love to have the money we don't.

So Jesus is a threat. Jesus tells us to give away our possessions. But we hold on to what we own, shouting, "Mine! Mine! Mine!"

Judgment

Read Mark 10:23-25. (Here's the camel!) What interpretations have you heard about the "eye of a needle"? What difference is there in the interpretation if we take Jesus' comment literally or figuratively? Since it is impossible for a camel to complete such a contortion and it's harder for a wealthy person to enter the Kingdom, is Jesus saying that it is beyond any possibility for a rich person to be saved?

Judgment

Jesus announces God's judgment in Mark 10:23-25: "How hard it will be for those who have wealth to enter the kingdom of God! . . . It is easier for a camel to go through the eye of a needle than for someone who is rich to enter the kingdom of God."

We try to comfort ourselves. "The eye of the needle is a rock formation or a small gate in the city wall," we say (but it isn't). "A camel can get through if it bends its neck and squeezes through." No, Jesus was talking about a real camel loaded down with riches and a real sewing needle with an eye too small to see. It's a funny idea. Think of a camel trying to squeeze through the eye of a needle, first one whisker, then another. Jesus played it for a laugh, but underneath the humor is judgment. Salvation is almost impossible for a rich person.

(Just a note: Economists appropriately use the CAMEL rating—capital, assets, management, earnings, liquidity—to determine the financial soundness of a bank!)

Read Mark 10:26-31. Jesus did not specifically answer the disciples' question except to say that none of us are saved by our own power; only by God for whom nothing is impossible. Since that is so, what difference does any of our behavior make concerning wealth (or anything else?)

The disciples questioned Jesus. "Who can be saved?" And Jesus answered, "For God all things are possible," which holds out the possibility for all to be saved (10:26-27). Jesus offers judgment and hope. God can save even the rich man who is caught up in his possessions and unable to give. God can save the world by overhauling the economic system. For God all things are possible.

We're relieved. Maybe judgment isn't the last word. Maybe we can hold onto our possessions after all.

Not so. God saves the rich by making them generous. God changes economic systems so they are based on loving neighbors. Salvation means that we will be changed, whether we like it or not. Jesus pronounces judgment on the rich: Give away your possessions, or they will be taken away.

God's judgment frightens us. Does God really favor the poor? Will the gates of heaven slam in our faces because we live comfortably?

The Rich Man and Lazarus

Read Luke 19:19-31 and summarize what happened. Who are the characters in the parable and what do they contribute to the story?

In small groups do two things: retell the story and add your own ending. Retell the story by having each member of the group tell a portion then pass to the next person. Do the same for the ending or else, when the retelling gets to the conclusion, sep-

The Rich Man and Lazarus

Read Luke 16:19-31.

A rich man lived in luxury, while Lazarus begged at his door. When they died, Lazarus was "carried away by the angels to be with Abraham." The rich man was tormented in a fiery hell. The rich man asked Abraham, "Send Lazarus to bring me cool water." (He was still giving orders!) But Abraham reminded him, "Child, remember that during your lifetime you received your good things, and Lazarus in like manner evil things; but now he is comforted here, and you are in agony." Again the rich man asked Abraham to send Lazarus to warn the man's brothers. But Abraham replied, "If they do not listen to Moses and the prophets, neither

arately write your own ending and compare them.

Bible 301 ☐

Read more about this parable in a Bible commentary. What is the significance of Abraham in the story?

What would you have Dives learn from your story? What did Jesus intend for his hearers to learn?

Review Bishop Trench's commentary. Explain why you agree or disagree with him. What is the message for us?

will they be convinced even if someone rises from the dead."

Lazarus was rewarded and the rich man condemned. The "symptom" was money—or the lack of it. But the heart of the issue was their position before God. The rich man, who is sometimes identified as Dives (a Latin translation that means "rich"), ignored his Torah obligation to the poor, toward whom God asks special care. The chasm between them was established. Dives should have listened.

Archbishop Richard Trench, writing of this parable at the turn of the twentieth century, summed up this point admirably: "The sin of Dives in its root is unbelief: hard-hearted contempt of the poor, luxurious squandering on self, are only the forms which his sin assumes. The seat of the disease is within; these are but the running sores which witness for the inward plague. He who believes not in an invisible world of righteousness and truth and spiritual joy, must place his hope in things which he sees, which he can handle, and taste, and smell. It is not the essence of the matter, whether he hoards [like the rich fool, 12:16-21] or squanders [like the prodigal son, 15:11-32]: in either case he puts his trust in the world" (quoted in *The New Interpreter's Bible*, Volume IX; Abingdon Press, 1995; page 319). "You cannot serve God and wealth," says Jesus, again and again.

Those who have wealth or who want wealth don't want to hear that. But Jesus asks for our wallets. And he tells us pointedly that, "Those who store up treasures for themselves . . . are not rich toward God" (12:21). It is hard, he says, for those who have wealth to enter the kingdom of God; in fact, the last will be first and the first last.

Jesus challenges our financial security, then threatens our hope of the Kingdom. Of course, he got in trouble!

Choices

Choices

Sing or read together the hymn "When I Survey the Wondrous Cross" (see particularly stanza 4) or "Amazing Grace" (particularly stanzas 4 and 5). What do these hymns convey about our salvation and our dependence on God? Is the message in those hymns just to be understood on a "spiritualized" level or does it have anything to do with the nuts and bolts of life, like the use of our resources? Explain.

Summarize the Gospel teaching for this session and consider again Matthew 6:33. Then respond to this statement following in light of Jesus' economic demands:

"They should in faithfulness to Christ and His gospel observe the right order of values in their earthly activities. Thus their whole lives, both individual and social, will be permeated with the spirit of the beatitudes, notably with the spirit of poverty.

"Whoever in obedience to Christ seeks first the kingdom of God will as a consequence receive a stronger and purer love for helping all his brothers

Jesus leaves us with a choice: We can give up our possessions, or we can continue to cling to them. Jesus says, "This very night your life is being demanded of you." Listen to the double meaning. The more obvious meaning is that we die, leaving behind bank accounts and computer systems and real estate. We can't take it with us. The other meaning, not so obvious, is that Jesus demands our lives today, not only to fit us for the future, but to participate in building the Kingdom now.

Jesus demands our all, including our possessions. Jesus says, "Follow me." Can we—like Peter, Andrew, James, John, Levi, and the rest—drop everything and follow? Jesus calls us to give up our possessions, even our livelihood. He says to us, "Go, sell what you have, and give the money to the poor . . . then come, follow me."

So one choice is to cash in all our bank accounts and stock options and to hold the ultimate garage sale. We can sell all we have, give the money to the poor, and follow Jesus. The other option is to keep our possessions. Mark says that the rich man, called to follow Jesus, "was shocked and went away grieving, for he had many possessions" (Mark 10:22). We can do the same. Jesus shocks us. We don't like to give away our money. Underneath greed is fear. If we give away our possessions and give up our jobs, how will we support ourselves? How will we eat? drink? How will we live?

We can walk away, like the rich man. Jesus

[and sisters] and for perfecting the work of justice under the inspiration of charity" ("*Gaudium et Spes:* Pastoral Constitution on the Church in the Modern World (Second Vatican Council, December 7, 1965)"; in *The Gospel of Peace and Justice*; Orbis Books, 1976; page 308).

offers us a choice: We can be disciples of Jesus Christ or we can keep our stuff. We can change or not.

Of course, if we hold on to what we own, God will eventually take it away. God will create an economic system based on loving neighbors, which will demand our generosity. Salvation means a new social, political, economic order in which wealth is redistributed and, as in the vision of the early church, all things are held in common (see Acts 2:43-47). God will change our priorities and redraw our budgets. If we are tight-fisted, holding on to our money, God will pry open our hands.

Jesus makes trouble by threatening our financial security. He says to us, "Give up all that you have and follow me." He lets us know that one way or another, the rich walk away empty-handed.

Close With Prayer

Consider all the choices you can make about the use of your financial resources, and pray for guidance to make the decisions and commitments to which you feel God is calling you. Close with the prayer: "God, lead us to choose your Kingdom, to commit our possessions to your use, and to follow Jesus Christ our Lord. Amen."

Session Seven

Jesus Challenges What We Consider Good

A Challenge

Jesus challenges the social order, wealth, apathy, secular and religious authority, and our attempts at discipleship. Jesus also challenges the underpinnings of society. Jesus questions what we consider good: "What is prized by human beings is an abomination in the sight of God" (Luke 16:15b).

What are the values that sustain our nation? We hear them in conversation: "What's most important is your family. You need to be responsible for your kids." Values turn up on the bumpers of our cars: "America: Home of the Free." They highlight political speeches: "Faith and Families," "Liberty and Justice." Consider the values we hold dear: patriotism, family, piety, justice. The values that undergird our society begin with life, liberty, and the pursuit of happiness.

We expect Jesus to question us, to condemn our materialism, our apathy, our shallow faith. But Jesus challenges what we consider good. He challenges our values.

Patriotism

We are citizens of a great nation, and we love our country. Patriotism is the foundation of American life. Because we love our

Session Focus

Jesus questions our values: patriotism, family, piety, justice. Jesus troubles us by offering a different understanding of life, liberty, and happiness.

Session Objective

To recognize that our values are open to question and to respond to Jesus' call to live for the sake of the gospel.

Session Preparation

You will need to have a picture book of Jesus, a Bible commentary, a Bible dictionary, a dictionary, and hymnals for the activities.

Choose from among these activities and discussion starters to plan your lesson.

A Challenge

Make a list of values important to our society. How might Jesus Christ challenge those values?

country, we'll fight for our way of life and we'll die for our freedom.

Jesus is not a patriot; he challenges our allegiance to our nation. Jesus ushered in a new and eschatological system that transcends the dailiness of nation, systems, order. As an "end time" people, other things become more important. The reconciliation of nations becomes of more concern than any one nation. "Mine" gives way to "ours" and to "God's."

When Jesus was brought to the Temple, Simeon took one look at him and prayed, "My eyes have seen your salvation, / which you have prepared in the presence of *all peoples*" (Luke 2:30-31, italics added).

John announced the arrival of the Messiah: "Prepare the way of the Lord, make his paths straight. / Every valley shall be filled, and every mountain and hill / shall be made low . . . / and *all flesh* shall see the salvation of God" (Luke 3:4b-6, italics added).

The Book of Revelation says of Jesus: "You were slaughtered and by your blood you ransomed for God / *saints from every tribe and language and people and nation*" (Revelation 5:9, italics added).

Jesus Christ was born and died for the people of all nations. Christ is salvation for Jews and Gentiles and also for the people of the United States and Uganda and Iran and Korea and South Africa and Brazil. God brings people of all nations together, kneeling at the manger and standing side by side at the foot of the cross.

Patriotism stands in opposition to God's salvation in Jesus Christ. Faith leaves no room for national allegiance. We are God's people. When we fight for our country, we go to battle against brothers and sisters whom Christ would have us love as friend

Patriotism ■

What does patriotism mean to you? In what ways do you express your allegiance to the United States?

Form three teams and divide among them Luke 2:30-31; Luke 3:5-6; and Revelation 5:9. Read enough of the surrounding verses to get the context and meaning of the passage. To whom were these texts addressed originally and what was their situation? What were their expectations concerning the present and the future age?

Bible 301 ☐

Use a Bible commentary to augment your understanding of these passages as necessary.

If you take seriously the idea that Jesus was born and died for all people, how will you change your opinions? your lifestyle? What are the practical implications of faith for foreign policy? for the international economy? for loving your neighbor?

Bible 301 ☐

Look at a variety of pictures of the birth of Christ and his crucifixion. Try to find pictures that represent art from several different nations. Notice the differ-

ences. We usually see pictures of Jesus as if he were European. How does the depiction of Jesus in other cultures affect and expand your appreciation of his universal ministry and how persons relate to and understand him?

rather than treat as enemy (whom we are called to love as well).

John might have announced the Messiah by saying, "Fill up the seas; lock continents together; tear down the customs offices and the checkpoints; flatten out the pride that separates nations so that all people will see God's salvation."

Jesus challenges patriotism.

Family

Draw a picture of your family. Write several words that describe your feelings about your family.

Family

Listen to the ways we talk about our families. "I have a job halfway across the country, but my mom sends E-mail every day." "I have to work to support my family; I wish I could spend more time with them." "I'm getting older; I have to decide what's most important in my life. I want to spend a lot of time with my grandchildren." "Families are the fabric of society."

Families are the most important people in our lives. But Jesus challenges our loyalties. "Whoever loves father or mother more than me is not worthy of me; and whoever loves son or daughter more than me is not worthy of me" (Matthew 10:37). Jesus is clear: Families are not as important as Jesus.

Read Matthew 4:22 and Luke 9:57-62. Imagine what it was like for the disciples to leave their families and their family responsibilities. How would you respond to Jesus' call? Would you be able to leave your family?

The context of Matthew is of an urgent sense of the coming of the Kingdom; we probably don't read or experience it that way. Does this mitigate Jesus' sense of urgency? of the

Jesus called disciples to leave their families, to turn their backs on parents and children and family responsibilities to follow him. And they did. Called to discipleship, James and John "immediately . . . left the boat and their father, and followed" (Matthew 4:22). The disciples followed without taking care of unfinished family business and without saying goodbye. Read Luke 9:57-62.

We try to gloss over Jesus' words. Faith, after all, is centered in the family. We go to church together. We pray together. We celebrate religious holidays together. Following

importance of dropping everything for the sake of the gospel? If so, how?

If we are called to put "the hand to the plow and not look back" who is supposed to care for family and other obligations? Does this imply that only one person in a household is a follower and that somehow the remaining family members are forfeit? If an element of discipleship is in love and service to our neighbor, then is the care of our family left to someone else's "neighborliness"? Discuss your responses.

Jesus is a family project. Surely, Jesus didn't really mean that we should leave our families.

But that's what he said. Jesus demands our total allegiance, and if family interferes with devotion to Christ, Jesus was clear about who comes first. Sometimes, family loyalty comes close to idolatry. Churches are packed on Mother's Day. Church school curriculum teaches young children, in the midst of its Bible stories, that one way of loving neighbors is by helping Mom with the dishes and being nice to siblings. If the lesson ends there, though, family values replace commandments, and family togetherness has replaced Christian fellowship. We will have confused our loyalties. So yes, Jesus does command us to leave our families and follow.

There's more. Jesus has a vision of what God wants for the world. God will create a new social order in which all people are family. Jesus announced, "My mother and my brothers are those who hear the word of God and do it" (Luke 8:21). And the Gospel of John talks about "children of God, who were born, not of blood or of the will of the flesh or of the will of man, but of God" (John 1:12-13). God will create a family.

Read John 1:12-13 and Matthew 10:34-39. How is "family" understood in these passages? How does the eschatological (end time) context of these passages affect their meaning and your understanding?

Jesus says that individual families will be destroyed so that God's family can be created. How do you feel about Jesus' words?

The portion of God's family to whom Matthew addressed his Gospel were predominantly Jewish Christians who were forging their way through the uncharted waters of the early Messianic community. Their belief in Christ was typically a point of division from their observant Jewish community, which doubtless included members of their families. Belief versus unbelief was doubtless a point of contention; perhaps sufficient basis to threaten the Christians' participation in synagogue observances. Matthew writes that Jesus warned his hearers of this potential division, but that the creation of a "family" of followers, especially in a community expecting the Kingdom, was paramount.

How do we get from a society based on families (plural) to a society that is God's family (singular)? Jesus answers (in Matthew 10:35-36): "I have come to set a man against his father, / and a daughter against her mother, / and a daughter-in-law against her mother-in-law; / and one's foes will be members of one's own household." Jesus challenges our allegiance to our families.

Piety

Piety

In what ways do you relate to God? In what ways do you love your neighbors? Is relating to neighbors more important than relating to God? How does Mark 12:33 influence how you understand the importance of worship (when the fourth commandment demands that we honor the sabbath and keep it)?

Define and discuss how you understand the meanings of *piety, worship, devotion, liturgy,* and *spirituality.* How do these practices, forms, and way of being work together to help us be the people of God in community and personally? How do they work together to help you understand God's will for your life?

In recent years, spirituality has staged a comeback. We're going to church and saying our prayers. We're searching for new ways to get in touch with God. A section of the newspaper is now devoted to religion, and headlines occasionally appear on the front page: "Priest Rediscovers Ancient Rites." "Local Church Rejoices in the Spirit."

Jesus questions our piety, asking, "Do you love your neighbors?" Loving neighbors is more important than empty liturgy. True piety is not heart-warming ritual but down-to-earth neighbor love. "Leave your gift there before the altar and go," says Jesus; "first be reconciled to your brother or sister, and then come and offer your gift" (Matthew 5:24). Loving God and neighbors is "much more important than all whole burnt offerings and sacrifices" (Mark 12:33).

Some of us prefer our piety to be solemn ritual, private and alone, as if worship was somehow apart from the community. Jesus doubts privatistic piety and calls us back to the commandment: Love God; love neighbors.

We call ourselves a Christian nation. We profess to be "one nation under God."

Perhaps we realize that spirituality is more than individuals opening themselves to God. Perhaps we believe that spirituality should be written in the laws of the land and form the foundation of our political, economic, social world. We cannot claim to be faithful when the poor live in cardboard homes and children are killed by stray bullets. Jesus sees our social-economic distinctions and doubts our piety.

Our constitution does not allow us to insist that all citizens see themselves as one nation under God, but our faith calls us to be Christian citizens. If we can't legislate that our convictions be codified into law, what can we do?

Prayer comes more easily than loving neighbors for many of us. Jesus challenges our new-found spirituality, which we thought was good. He asks, "What are you doing with your knees bent and your heads bowed? What are you doing with candles and sweet music? Remember to get off your knees and serve your neighbors." Like the prophet Micah, Jesus lets us know that God wants our public worship and private devotion to prompt us to action. God expects us "to do justice, and to love kindness, and to walk humbly" with God (Micah 6:8).

Justice for All ■

Consider the definitions of *justice* as they are used in common conversation. Are they the same as the biblical understanding of justice?

Bible 301 □

Using a Bible dictionary, look up justice. *What new understandings emerge?*

Justice for All

What does *justice* mean? The dictionary offers several definitions: Justice is fairness. Justice is a system of reward and punishment established by law. Justice is also righteousness, conformity to truth or to God's will or to moral law. To establish justice means to make things right.

When we think of justice, we're apt to think of the legal system: courts of law, attorneys, defendants, juries. Justice has to do with judgment. Conventional wisdom understands justice as taking criminals off the streets. We talk about society's need to "see justice done." Justice, in some minds, is a ten-foot-square cell with a pail in the corner or a flicker of lights, a jolt of electricity, a man fried. "An eye for an eye," we say, quoting Scripture. *This*, we think, *is God's will.*

Jesus answers, "You have heard that it was said, 'An eye for an eye and a tooth for a tooth.' But I say to you, Do not resist an evildoer. But if anyone strikes you on the right cheek, turn the other also" (Matthew 5:38-39).

What is the difference between "judge not" and the judgments and decisions you routinely make everyday? How can we live without using our judgment? Is that what "judge not" means? How do discernment, reconciliation and transformation fit in here?

Jesus challenges our understanding of justice. For him, justice is righteousness. Jesus looks at our society from God's point of view and calls us to conform to God's will. "Judge not," says Jesus, "for only God can judge." "Do not judge other people, but see your own sin and repent." Jesus wants us to think in new ways, to establish *God's* justice, which isn't "an eye for eye," but "pure, unbounded love." God is merciful. Reconciliation and transformation is the godly goal, not retribution and punishment.

A young man was killed in a drive-by shooting. When his killer came to trial, his mother refused to ask for the death penalty. "After all," she said, "he has a mother too." The boy was convicted and sentenced. Every week his mother and the victim's mother visited him in prison. And when he got out, they helped him finish school and find a job. Mercy.

Identify issues of criminal justice and also issues that affect people who have "no voice and no money and no power." What laws are being discussed in Congress? Consider: How would Jesus vote? What position would he take? What laws express God's mercy?

Not only does Jesus question our understanding of crime and punishment, he also challenges our sense of fairness and equal treatment under the law. God's justice is the original plan for affirmative action. When Old Testament prophets called for justice, they meant that the courts of law should not be objective; they should side with the helpless, with people who had no voice and no money and no power. Jesus asks for more: good news for the poor, freedom for the oppressed, release for the prisoners (Luke

4:18; see Isaiah 61:1-2). Justice, for Jesus, is not crime and punishment or equality or even fairness, but mercy.

Jesus said, "If you had known what this means, "I desire mercy and not sacrifice," you would not have condemned the guiltless" (Matthew 12:7). Perhaps Jesus was talking about himself, the sacrifice, innocent and condemned in the name of justice. Jesus challenges our understanding of justice.

The Basics

In what tangible ways do you understand the US to be based on the freedom to pursue life, liberty, and happiness?

Bible 301

Sing or read together one of the patriotic hymns in your hymnal. What do the words suggest about the sovereignty of God and country? About a "nation under God"?

The Basics

Our nation was founded on the right to life, liberty, and the pursuit of happiness. They are the basics of life in the United States, and they are good. The "American dream" is that anyone can "pull himself up by his bootstraps" and attain whatever goals he or she sets. We have a great nation, built on principles that are good.

Jesus challenges what we consider good. He questions both our understanding and our pursuit of life, liberty, and happiness.

Happiness

Form groups of three. Imagine that the magical genie has popped out of the bottle to grant each of you your three wishes. What would you wish for? Would this make you happy?

Then imagine that there was no limit to what wish can be granted; you can have anything, tangible or intangible, that you want. What would you ask for and in what order? How selfish or altruistic is your wish list? How would your life be different? In the

Happiness

The MC of the quiz show walked through the television audience, asking, "What will make *you* happy?" Prospective contestants shouted, "a new car," "a million dollars," "a Caribbean cruise." Things make us happy. Of course, some of us would prefer power, acceptance, or fame; our role models are celebrities: actresses in tinsel gowns, athletes slick with sweat. Some of us want only health, a long life, security, well-adjusted children, a comfortable home. What will make us happy? All of us want our lives to be full and our dreams fulfilled.

We pursue happiness. We move from job to job climbing the corporate ladder. We exercise and diet and read self-help books.

long run, would it be better? In what ways do you pursue happiness?

Read what Malcolm Muggeridge says about the pursuit of happiness. When have you been disillusioned by the pursuit of happiness? When has happiness seemed like an illusion?

We fill our conversation with cheerful platitudes. We do our best to be happy.

Malcolm Muggeridge said in a radio broadcast, "The pursuit of happiness is responsible for a good part of the ills and miseries of the modern world. . . . The pursuit of happiness in any case soon resolved itself into the pursuit of pleasure—something quite different. Pleasure is but a mirage of happiness—a false vision of shade and refreshment seen across parched sand" (*Muggeridge Through the Microphone*, 1967).

Pursuing happiness, if confined to pleasure-seeking, is disappointing at best. The gospel holds out a different image of happiness, quite apart from pleasure. Pursuing happiness is also a contradiction in terms. Happiness is given by God; it's a blessing.

Read the Beautitudes aloud. Compare the translation in the New Revised Standard Version with the translation in The Good News Bible (TEV). When "happiness" is understood as a beatified life, how does that differ from the way happiness is typically understood? How is happiness exhibited when it is a characteristic of a sanctified life?

Read the Beatitudes in Matthew 5:1-11. The Good News Bible (TEV) translates the word *blessed* as "happy," although *blessed* better addresses what this term means. *Makarismos*, from the root *makar* (blessed), refers to beatification; a sanctification by God. Blessedness is different from what we typically mean by happiness.

Blessedness is for those who love God and neighbor; those who are blessed are humble, merciful. They do what God requires; they make peace. Jesus' picture of blessedness is a far cry from our unsatisfying search for pleasure and self-fulfillment. Those who are blessed realize they are "poor in spirit" and that their spirit rests in God. As a result, they turn to God and love their neighbors. Blessed are those who *do not* pursue happiness. Happiness is a gift, a blessing.

Have you disregarded your neighbors in order to pursue your own happiness? If you yearn for blessedness

The commandments challenge our individual hankerings for personal fulfillment. How can we love our neighbors when we're busy working for a bigger house in a better neighborhood? Neighbors have little place in our lives, except perhaps to applaud our efforts at slimming down, to keep the kids while we enjoy a few days at the beach, to provide competition in the most-closely-clipped-yard-in-town contest. We don't even think about faraway neighbors who are dying of starvation or losing their families to AIDS. Just thinking about neighbors in trouble makes us unhappy!

But Jesus is not too concerned with our personal happiness; he expects us to yearn for blessedness and to love our neighbors, regardless of whether we're happy or fulfilled.

and rest your spirit in God's Spirit, will you automatically be happy? Why or why not?

Liberty

In the United States, we're guaranteed freedom of religion, of the press, of speech, of assembly; freedom from discrimination; freedom to be ourselves. "Freedom" is our rallying cry.

Of course, liberty isn't absolute. My freedom ends where yours begins. When we encroach on the freedom of others, laws are passed and courts are called to order. But within limits—and the limits are broad—we can do as we please.

Christian faith is all about liberty. God set free the slaves in Egypt and made them God's children. God brought home the Israelites exiled in Babylon. Through Jesus Christ, God sets us free from sin. God forgives us and makes us God's own people.

Christian freedom makes American liberty look tame. Listen to Scripture:

"He disarmed the rulers and authorities . . . triumphing over them. . . . If with Christ you died to the elemental spirits of the universe, . . . why do you submit to regulations?" (Colossians 2:15, 20).

***Liberty* ■**

Write a declaration of independence, stating your freedom from social principles and your freedom for obedience. Be specific. What does it mean to live free in Christ?

***Bible 301* □**

Look up freedom *in a Bible dictionary. How are we freed, and from what are we freed?*

Review the various Scripture passages from Colossians, Romans, and Galatians, including enough of the surrounding text to get the context and full meaning of the passage. How does Paul characterize Christian freedom?

"Christ Jesus has set you free from the law of sin and of death. . . . The creation itself will be set free from its bondage to decay and will obtain the freedom of the glory of the children of God" (Romans 8:2, 21).

How do you experience your Christian faith as freeing you from the "elemental spirits of the universe"? What does that expression mean?

In Christ, we are free from rules and regulations and customs and the authority of government and yes, even the authority of the church. We are free from "elemental spirits," which can be understood both as the supernatural powers of evil or as the underlying principles of human society: the spirits of exclusiveness, greed, power, insecurity, hedonism, fear, one-upmanship, selfishness, pride. In Christ, we are free from sin and death. Isn't it amazing? Christ has set us free from just about everything. We can shout and sing with the saints, "For freedom Christ has set us free" (Galatians 5:1)!

Does this mean we are no longer bound by the ground rules of society? Without rules or convention, what happens next?

Bible 301 ☐

Read Romans 6:15-23 and a commentary on this text in a bible commentary. How is being a "slave to God" sanctifying? Do you regard yourself as a slave to God? This kind of "slavery" actually offers radical freedom. How can that be? In what ways would you recognize that "slavery" or radical freedom? Is this something you want? Why or why not?

Read Romans 6:15-23. The Bible says, "Thanks be to God that you, having once been slaves of sin, have become obedient from the heart to the form of teaching to which you were entrusted" (Romans 6:17). We are free from sin and from the rules and regulations of society. But Christ is Lord. Christ has ultimate authority over our lives. Freedom in Christ is obedience. Jesus calls us to learn his teachings about the kind of world God wants for us. Jesus sets us free to leave our families, to give away our possessions, to establish justice and righteousness, to turn upside down our social world, to stand on the side of the helpless and the poor, to pray for the nations, to live with brothers and sisters in peace. Christ sets us free to be a blessing to our neighbors, which must include our families, in order to demonstrate the grace of God.

Jesus offered a new set of values. They got him in trouble. Obedience will get us in trouble. Freedom is a pretty frightening proposition.

Life

Jesus healed the sick and raised the dead. He preached God's kingdom, where death will be no more and everyone will live with God. He promised new, abundant life. Clearly Jesus cherished the lives of people he met.

On the other hand, Jesus called his followers to give up their lives.

Read Mark 8:31-38. Jesus announced that he would suffer and die and be raised again. After all, he had threatened the people and got in trouble with both the religious and the secular authorities. Jesus would be executed in the name of justice, piety, power.

Peter took him aside and questioned him. We can imagine what Peter said. "Jesus, you don't have to die. Life is sacred. Don't throw away your life trying to change what you can't change." And Jesus answered, "You are setting your mind not on divine things but on human things" (8:33). Doing God's will is more important than life itself.

Then Jesus said, "If any want to become my followers, let them deny themselves and take up their cross and follow me. For those who want to save their life will lose it, and those who lose their life for my sake, and for the sake of the gospel, will save it" (Mark 8:34-35).

Taking up our cross is not the same as suffering through the usual daily aches and pains. It's not putting up with difficult neighbors or dealing with financial ruin. Taking up

***Life* ■**

Jesus doesn't deny our right to life, but suggests that obedience is more important. Jesus gave up his life by questioning the values of society and religion.

What does it mean to be obedient? In what ways would obeying God get us in trouble?

Read Mark 8:31-38. The cost of discipleship is high, but the rewards are great. To embrace this radical discipleship requires us to keep our minds on "divine things." What does it mean to "take up the cross"? to keep your mind on "divine things"? to "lose your life for the sake of the gospel" and thus, save it?

***Bible 301* □**

Look up some of your favorite hymns under "Discipleship and Service" in the hymnal index. Sing or read them together. How do they help encourage you to "take up your cross"?

our cross is giving up our lives to obedience. It means saying the same kinds of things that got Jesus crucified: "Woe to the rich and the powerful." "Christ saves sinners, not the righteous." "Be merciful, as God is merciful." And it means hanging out with sinners and outcasts, lobbying for changes in government so that the poor are fed and the helpless find a voice, giving up possessions. Taking up our cross means getting in trouble.

Maybe Jesus didn't value life as much as we do. Or maybe Jesus understood life to mean something different from what we do. More important than life is risking our lives for the sake of the gospel, for the sake of loving God and neighbors.

No wonder Jesus got in trouble!

Close With Prayer

Consider the yearning you have for God and the calls to "take up your cross." What might God be calling you to do or to be that will demonstrate God's grace in a needy world? How does God challenge your values and lift you from a search for happiness to a life of blessedness? Take these insights to God and close with a prayer for obedience and courage to lead a sanctified life.